LOW GI
food for friends

LOW GI
food for friends

hamlyn

Azmina Govindji

First published in Great Britain in 2006 by Hamlyn,
a division of Octopus Publishing Group Ltd
2–4 Heron Quays, London E14 4JP

ISBN-13: 978-0-600-61404-3
ISBN-10: 0-600-61404-2

A CIP catalogue record for this book is available from the
British Library

Printed and bound in China

10 9 8 7 6 5 4 3 2 1

Notes

Nutritional analyses are given per serving. Where a recipe
has split servings (e.g. 'serves 6–8'), the analysis is given for
the first figure.

The Department of Health advises that eggs should not be
consumed raw. This book contains some dishes made with
raw or lightly cooked eggs. It is prudent for more vulnerable
people, such as pregnant and nursing mothers, invalids, the
elderly, babies, and young children, to avoid uncooked or
lightly cooked dishes made with eggs.

Both metric and imperial measurements have been given.
Use one set of measurements only, not a mixture of both.

Standard level spoon measurements are used in all recipes.

1 tablespoon = one 15 ml spoon

1 teaspoon = one 5 ml spoon

Fresh herbs should be used unless otherwise stated.

Where pepper is listed in the recipe ingredients, always use
freshly ground black pepper.

Medium eggs should be used unless otherwise stated.

Ovens should be preheated to the specified temperature –
if using a fan-assisted oven, follow the manufacturer's
instructions for adjusting the time and the temperature.

The information in this book should not be considered
as a replacement for professional medical advice: a
physician should be consulted in all matters relating to
health and especially in relation to any symptoms that
may require diagnosis or medical attention.

CONTENTS

INTRODUCTION

You've probably picked up this book because you've heard a little about GI – glycaemic index – and want to embrace the health benefits a low-GI diet can offer, even when you're entertaining and indulging yourself a little. You may be interested in GI because you or someone close to you has developed diabetes and you are aware of the beneficial effects GI has on blood sugar or glucose levels. Or, possibly, you have just flicked through the pages that follow and noticed the enticing recipes and helpful nutritional notes. Whatever the reason for your interest, choosing low-GI foods can promote a healthy lifestyle, for you, your friends and your family.

Before we think about why the idea of GI is valuable when you are watching your health or your waistline, we need to know what GI actually means.

The glycaemic index is all about what happens to your food once it's left your fork. When you eat carbohydrate (such as bread, potatoes, pasta, cereals and sugary foods) your body digests it and converts it to glucose (sugar), which can be used for energy. As the carbohydrate gets converted to glucose, the glucose level in your blood rises. GI is simply a ranking of carbohydrate foods based on the speed at which they raise blood glucose or sugar levels after they have been digested. Each food is given a value:

- Carbs that break down quickly are given high values: they raise blood glucose quickly and have a high GI.
- Carbs that break down slowly are given low values: they raise blood glucose slowly and have a low GI.

Low-GI carbs, such as wholegrains, beans, lentils, pasta, nuts, seeds, fruit

and vegetables, are inherently healthy, and experts agree that these foods can make a valuable contribution to your diet. You don't need to know the GI ratings or values of individual foods in order to eat the low-GI way. Simply choose to have a low-GI food at each meal or snack, swapping your usual foods for the lower-GI versions as often as you can (see the lists on page 10 for some ideas).

The recipes that follow will give you plenty of ideas for meals using low-GI ingredients. They are designed to be easy to make and include bought ingredients, such as olives in herb-flavoured brine and ready-crushed ginger, that will save you time but give delicious results. To save you even more time we have also included some menu suggestions (see page 11) which will help you to combine the dishes within the book for various occasions, including a Summer lunch alfresco for six, a Sunday lunch for four and a Winter warmer for six.

THE FUSS ABOUT GI

When your blood glucose rises your body releases a hormone – insulin – from the pancreas. Insulin reduces your blood glucose levels by directing glucose from the blood either to your muscles (where it can be used for energy) or to fat stores (where it is stored as fuel for another time). The more quickly a food raises blood glucose levels, the higher its GI rating and the greater the insulin response. Research has suggested that if your blood glucose levels are constantly high, your blood insulin levels are consequently high, and this can lead to a condition known as insulin resistance (IR). IR can make you more prone to metabolic syndrome (Syndrome X), type-2 diabetes and coronary heart disease, especially if you are overweight. This is one of the key reasons why low-GI foods and meals can help you keep in good overall health.

Imagine eating a slice of multigrain bread. You have to chew the grains first, which takes more time than if you were to chew white or even wholemeal bread. The multigrain bread is also digested more slowly than white and wholemeal breads. This affects the speed at which they raise blood glucose. As a result, the GI rating of seeded breads, such as multigrain, are lower than – and preferable to – white and even wholemeal bread. Wholemeal is, of course, a better source of fibre than white bread, but in terms of GI it acts in pretty much the same way as white.

Blood glucose levels respond differently to high and low-GI foods. With a high-GI food the rapid rise in blood glucose is followed by a quick fall, which is associated with hunger. So, low-GI foods may actually help prevent hunger pangs – which is great news if you are watching your weight.

HOW TO GI YOUR DINNER TABLE

Identifying the GI of foods requires specific laboratory analysis, and not all foods have been analysed, even if they do contain carbs. If we were to assess the GI values of the recipes in this book, we would get an accurate measure only if we were to feed a group of people a measured amount of each dish. We would then, under laboratory conditions, test their blood glucose response over a period of time and compare this to the same amount of carbohydrate found in pure glucose – an expensive, laborious and unnecessary process! To keep it simple, these recipes have been carefully designed to include a selection of tasty yet low- to medium-GI ingredients. The way a dish is cooked, how long it's cooked for, what it is served with, whether you squeeze some lemon juice on top and more will affect the GI of the food. This knowledge has been carefully integrated into the recipes.

You will see that many of the recipes are dressed in lemon or lime juice or have a scattering of sesame seeds or a handful of nuts, all of which help to lower the GI of the finished dish.

In order that these recipes are super-tasty yet nutritious, you'll notice that they use reduced-fat ingredients, such as Greek yogurt instead of cream, lean meats and better-for-you mono-unsaturated oils, such as olive and rapeseed oil.

So, go on, treat yourself – and your friends – to one of my scrumptious, nutritious, low-GI gourmet meals any day of the week!

Low-GI foods

Eat the following foods often – they are your best friends:

- **Grainy breads,** such as multigrain, soya and linseed and softgrain white

- **Porridge and muesli**

- **Pasta** – any type – cooked until *al dente* and smothered in tomato-based sauce (even a basic one from a jar)

- **Veggies galore** – raw ones are best, but if you're cooking keep them firm

- **Fruits,** especially apples, pears (even canned ones in natural juice), strawberries and peaches

- **Basmati rice, sweet potato, couscous and new potatoes cooked in their skins**

- **Beans** – choose from kidney beans, chickpeas, baked beans and lentils; even canned chilli beans get a GI gold star

- **Lean meat, fish and poultry;** eat egg, Quorn™, tofu and nuts if you prefer vegetarian main meals

- **Nuts** (yes nuts!) – have a handful a day to help you manage your weight and lower your blood cholesterol levels

GI swaps for breakfast

Instead of this ... →	... have this
• Cornflakes, rice-based cereals, sugar-rich cereals	• Branflakes, cereals with dried fruit, oat-based cereals, such as porridge and muesli
• White or wholemeal bread	• Multigrain or other seeded bread
• Fruit juice	• Fresh fruit, such as grapefruit
• Jam	• Peanut butter

GI swaps for lunch

Instead of this ... →	... have this
• Baguette or bagel, wholemeal or white bread	• Granary bread, wheat tortilla wrap, rye bread, pitta bread, multigrain bread
• Hummus	• Chickpea salad
• Potato salad	• Pasta salad
• Puréed soup	• Soup with whole beans or lentils

GI swaps for dinner

Instead of this ... →	... have this
• Roast or mashed potato	• Boiled new potatoes in their skins
• Jasmine or risotto rice	• Basmati, brown or long-grain rice
• Sweet or oily dressing	• Acidic dressing based on lime or lemon juice
• Baked potato	• Baked yam, cassava or sweet potato

GI swaps for snacks

Instead of this ... →	... have this
• Chocolate bar	• A handful of nuts
• Rich dessert	• Fruit, yogurt, dried fruit, regular ice cream
• Digestive biscuits, cream crackers or rice cakes	• Oatcakes, oat-based biscuits
• Cake	• Fruit loaf or currant bun

MENU SUGGESTIONS

Meal for two

Grilled Haloumi with Sun-dried Tomatoes (see page 22)

Seared Tuna with Lemon Salsa (see page 47)

Garlic, Roasted Pepper and Walnut Pappardelle (see page 84)

Sizzling Bananas with Orange Rind and Pistachios (see page 138)

Summer lunch alfresco for six

Salmon Mousse on Pumpernickel (see page 16)

Rosemary Lamb Shanks with Red Onions and Spiced Beans (see page 55)

Caramelized French Beans (see page 114)

Chinese Spiced Citrus Salad (see page 130)

After-work supper with friends for six

Buttered Asparagus Spears with Toasted Sesame Seeds (see page 27)

Lemon Sole with Butter and Dill (see page 38)

Fragrant Cinnamon Basmati Rice (see page 112)

Sautéed Okra with Onion Seeds and Saffron (see page 119)

Bitter Chocolate Almond Mousse (see page 128)

Winter warmer for six

Cauliflower Cheese Soup with Toasted Pumpkin Seeds (see page 14)

Braised Oxtail with Orange (see page 74)

Almond and Apricot Wild Rice with Cumin Seeds (see page 91)

Ginger Broccoli with Fennel Seeds (see page 109)

Baked Pear with Almond Crumble (see page 124)

Sunday lunch for four

Stuffed Garlic Mushrooms with Feta Cheese (see page 25)

Plaice en Papillotte with Fennel and Chilli (see page 51)

Fruity Couscous with Lime (see page 116)

Cherry and Macadamia Granola (see page 126)

Family supper for four

Beef Tikka with Tamarind Dipping Sauce (see page 24)

Japanese-style Salmon Steaks (see page 46)

Stir-fried Noodles with Field Mushrooms (see page 101)

Baked Saffron Peaches with Mango and Cream (see page 136)

Sensational Starters

CAULIFLOWER CHEESE SOUP
with toasted pumpkin seeds

Preparation time: 15–20 minutes

Cooking time: 1¼ hours

Serves 6

2 tablespoons vegetable oil

1 onion, finely chopped

1 large cauliflower, about 1.2 kg (2½ lb), cut into florets

50 g (2 oz) strong Cheddar cheese, grated

black pepper

VEGETABLE STOCK

500 g (1 lb) mixed vegetables (excluding potatoes, parsnips and other starchy root vegetables), chopped

1 garlic clove, thinly sliced

6 peppercorns

1 bouquet garni

1.2 litres (2 pints) water

TO SERVE

2 tablespoons pumpkin seeds

4 tablespoons reduced-fat fromage frais

CARBOHYDRATE 9 g

FAT 9 g

PROTEIN 12 g

ENERGY 168 kcal/698 kJ

1 Make the vegetable stock. Put all the ingredients in a large saucepan. Bring to the boil and simmer gently for 30 minutes, skimming if necessary. Strain the stock through a muslin-lined sieve, return to the saucepan and keep warm. These ingredients will make about 1 litre (1¾ pints), and any stock not used in this recipe can be chilled then frozen for use in other dishes.

2 Meanwhile, heat the oil in a large saucepan and fry the onion. Cook gently until it is soft but not browned. Add the cauliflower florets, cover and cook for 5–10 minutes. Stir in 900 ml (1½ pints) of the vegetable stock and simmer for 30 minutes until the cauliflower is tender.

3 Lightly toast the pumpkin seeds in a dry, nonstick frying pan. They will start to pop when they are ready, but keep watch as they cook because they can easily burn.

4 Purée the soup in a food processor or rub through a sieve and return it to the saucepan. Add the cheese and season with black pepper. Reheat thoroughly until the cheese melts through the soup. If wished, add more liquid, such as hot stock or vegetable water to thin the soup.

5 Serve in warm bowls with a swirl of fromage frais and a sprinkle of toasted pumpkin seeds.

Nutrition notes

The pumpkin seeds add a crunchy texture as well as being a good source of minerals and healthy omega-3 fats.

Choosing a strong cheese helps you to use less and also reduces the need for extra salt.

SALMON MOUSSE
on pumpernickel

Preparation time: 25 minutes, plus setting

Serves 8

450 g (14½ oz) poached salmon,
any bones removed

50 g (2 oz) reduced-fat crème fraîche

150 g (5 oz) reduced-fat fromage frais

1 tablespoon chopped dill, plus extra dill
leaves for garnish

4 tablespoons lemon juice

1 egg white

15 g (½ oz) leaf gelatine (about 4 sheets)

1 teaspoon vegetable oil

black pepper

mixed salad leaves, to garnish

TO SERVE

4 slices dark pumpernickel bread, quartered

4 lemons, cut into wedges

CARBOHYDRATE 9 g

FAT 10 g

PROTEIN 16 g

ENERGY 190 kcal/798 kJ

1 In a large bowl, flake the salmon and then beat in the crème fraîche, fromage frais, dill, lemon juice and black pepper. Mix well.

2 Whisk the egg white until peaks form. Melt the gelatine in 3–4 tablespoons very hot, but not boiling, water. Stir the gelatine into the fish mixture and then carefully fold in the egg white.

3 Coat the insides of 8 moulds or ramekin dishes with a little oil to prevent the mousse from sticking. Spoon the fish mixture into the moulds or ramekin dishes, cover with clingfilm and place in the refrigerator for 2–3 hours to set.

4 Remove the mousse from the moulds or ramekin dishes by sliding a knife around the edges to loosen, then turn them upside down.

5 Garnish with the extra dill leaves and some mixed salad leaves and serve with quarters of pumpernickel bread and lemon wedges.

Poaching salmon Use a large piece of salmon, such as the tail end. Put the salmon in a large pan or fish kettle, add a bay leaf, parsley sprigs, a bouquet garni, 10 whole black peppercorns and water to cover. Bring to simmering point and cook for 2 minutes. Turn off the heat and leave, covered, to cool. The residual heat in the water will poach the salmon. Do not remove the lid until it is completely cool (at least 5 hours). Lift the salmon from the poaching liquor and remove any skin and bones.

Nutrition notes

Pumpernickel bread has a lower GI than other breads, and its flavour marries well with oily fish.

Fresh salmon is a wonderful source of omega-3 fatty acids, which help to lower blood triglycerides, a risk factor in heart disease.

PANEER CUBES
with cumin and baby spinach

Preparation time: 5 minutes

Cooking time: 3–4 minutes

Serves 4

1 tablespoon rapeseed oil

2 teaspoons cumin seeds

200 g (7 oz) Indian paneer cheese, cut into
1 cm (½ inch) cubes

¼ teaspoon ground turmeric

¼ teaspoon paprika

60 g (2½ oz) baby spinach leaves

juice of 1 lime

salt and black pepper

CARBOHYDRATE 1 g

FAT 19 g

PROTEIN 5 g

ENERGY 191 kcal/800 kJ

1 Heat the oil in a nonstick wok or frying pan and add the cumin seeds. Allow them to pop over a low heat for a few seconds.

2 Stir in the cheese, turmeric and paprika, season to taste and cook for 3–4 minutes until lightly browned.

3 Toss the cheese mixture with the spinach and lime juice and serve immediately.

Nutrition note

Although it is sometimes called cottage cheese in Indian restaurants, paneer is actually a high-fat cheese, so don't go overboard on this one!

HONEYED FIGS
with raspberries and goats' cheese

Preparation time: 3 minutes

Cooking time: 3 minutes

Serves 4–8

8 fresh figs, preferably black

1 tablespoon clear honey

125 g (4 oz) raspberries

75 g (3 oz) reduced-fat goats' cheese,
cut into 4 thin slices

a handful of flat leaf parsley, chopped,
to garnish

CARBOHYDRATE 17 g

FAT 3 g

PROTEIN 4 g

ENERGY 108 kcal/460 kJ

1 Halve the figs, put them in a foil-lined grill pan and drizzle the centre of each with a drop of honey. Cook under a preheated hot grill for 2–3 minutes.

2 Garnish with the flat leaf parsley and serve hot on individual plates alongside the goats' cheese and the raspberries.

Nutrition note

This tempting starter contributes one portion towards your recommended five-a-day fruit and vegetable intake.

HOT CHICKEN LIVER SALAD

Preparation time: 5 minutes, plus soaking

Cooking time: 5 minutes

Serves 4

400 g (13 oz) chicken livers, trimmed and halved

60 ml (2½ fl oz) milk

2 teaspoons thyme leaves

1 tablespoon olive oil

2 garlic cloves, crushed

1 red chilli pepper, sliced thinly (optional)

200 g (7 oz) can water chestnuts, drained and halved

TO SERVE

200 g (7 oz) chicory, leaves separated

1½–2 tablespoons balsamic vinegar

CARBOHYDRATE 9 g

FAT 10 g

PROTEIN 21 g

ENERGY 199 kcal/835 kJ

1 Soak the liver in milk for 30 minutes to remove any bitterness. Discard the milk and pat the liver dry with kitchen paper. Sprinkle the chopped thyme over both sides of the liver.

2 Heat the oil in a large frying pan and add the garlic and sliced chilli, if using. Allow the garlic and chilli to soften for 30 seconds and then add the chicken livers and water chestnuts.

3 Cook over a medium heat for 3–4 minutes, until the liver is browned on the outside but still pink in the middle.

4 Serve on bed of crispy raw chicory, drizzled with balsamic vinegar and with any remaining pan juices.

Nutrition note

Chicken livers are an excellent source of iron, protein and B vitamins.

GRILLED HALOUMI
with sun-dried tomatoes

Preparation time: 5 minutes

Cooking time: 10 minutes

Serves 4

200 g (7 oz) haloumi cheese, sliced

2 teaspoons onion seeds

1 tablespoon finely chopped coriander leaves

a few saffron threads

TO SERVE

20 g (¾ oz) sun-dried tomatoes in oil, drained and sliced

½ orange, peeled and pith removed, separated into segments

2 tablespoons lemon juice

rocket leaves, to garnish

CARBOHYDRATE 3 g

FAT 15 g

PROTEIN 11 g

ENERGY 186 kcal/778 kJ

1 Place the cheese slices on a foil-lined grill pan and sprinkle over the onion seeds, coriander leaves and saffron.

2 Preheat the grill and cook the cheese under a moderate heat for 4–5 minutes on each side until it is soft and slightly browned.

3 Serve immediately on a bed of sliced sun-dried tomatoes and orange segments. Drizzle the lemon juice over the cheese just before serving, and garnish with a few rocket leaves.

Nutrition notes

Tomatoes are a rich source of the antioxidant lycopene, which is known for its anti-cancer properties.

Haloumi cheese is naturally high in salt, so there is no need to add any extra in this recipe.

BEEF TIKKA
with tamarind dipping sauce

Preparation time: 10 minutes, plus marinating

Cooking time: 5 minutes

Serves 4

150 ml (¼ pint) reduced-fat natural yogurt

1½ tablespoons tandoori spice mix

300 g (10 oz) beef steak, cut into 2 cm (1 inch) cubes

2 teaspoons vegetable oil

½ teaspoon onion seeds

1 teaspoon crushed ginger

2 tablespoons chopped coriander leaves

DIPPING SAUCE

1 teaspoon tamarind paste

3 tablespoons warm water

1 tablespoon chopped coriander leaves

2 teaspoons finely chopped chives

½ teaspoon red chilli powder

salt and black pepper

CARBOHYDRATE 5 g

FAT 6 g

PROTEIN 18 g

ENERGY 140 kcal/590 kJ

1 Mix together the yogurt and tandoori spice mix and marinate the beef in the mixture for 30 minutes.

2 Meanwhile, make the dipping sauce by mixing together all the ingredients. Season to taste.

3 Heat the oil in a frying pan and add the onion seeds. Allow them to pop over a low heat for a few seconds. Stir in the ginger and add the marinated beef together with any juices.

4 Cook for about 5 minutes until the meat is just tender. Stir in the coriander leaves. Serve immediately accompanied by the dipping sauce.

Nutrition note
Yogurt and tandoori mixes can be used as a low-fat way of spicing up fish and chicken dishes too.

STUFFED GARLIC MUSHROOMS
with feta cheese

Preparation time: 10–12 minutes

Cooking time: 20 minutes

Serves 4

4 large field or portobello mushrooms

2 teaspoons olive oil

1 small onion, finely chopped

2 garlic cloves, crushed

60 g (2½ oz) feta cheese, finely diced

1 tablespoon chopped coriander leaves and stems

1 tablespoon chopped basil leaves

8 pitted olives, halved

black pepper

mixed salad leaves, to serve

CARBOHYDRATE 2 g

FAT 5 g

PROTEIN 3 g

ENERGY 67 kcal/276 kJ

1 Peel and remove the stalks from the mushrooms. Finely chop the stalks and sauté them in hot oil in a frying pan with the onion and garlic for 3–4 minutes until soft.

2 Mix the feta with the mushroom and onion mixture, add the herbs and season with black pepper.

3 Arrange the mushroom caps, flat side down, on a greased baking sheet and spoon the onion mixture on the top.

4 Lay the olives on top of this and cook in a preheated oven, 180°C (350°F), Gas Mark 4, for 20 minutes until browned. Serve immediately on a bed of mixed salad leaves.

Nutrition note

Feta cheese is naturally salty, so there is no need to add extra salt to this recipe.

BUTTERED ASPARAGUS SPEARS

with toasted sesame seeds

Preparation time: 3–5 minutes

Cooking time: about 15 minutes

Serves 6

500 g (1 lb) asparagus spears

1 tablespoon olive oil

25 g (1 oz) butter

4 teaspoons sesame seeds

1 teaspoon wholegrain mustard

CARBOHYDRATE 2 g

FAT 8 g

PROTEIN 3 g

ENERGY 90 kcal/372 kJ

1 Snap off any woody asparagus stems by bending the end of the spears. Heat the oil and butter in a flat, heavy-based frying pan.

2 Place asparagus spears in the pan in a single layer to cover the base of the pan and cook for about 5 minutes, until just tender and slightly charred. You may have to cook the asparagus in several batches.

3 Meanwhile, heat a nonstick frying pan and toast the sesame seeds for a few seconds, turning them with a wooden spoon until they start to brown.

4 Stir the mustard into the asparagus and serve immediately, topped with the toasted sesame seeds.

Nutrition note

One serving will give you almost three-quarters of your daily requirement of folate, a B vitamin. Folate, or folic acid, helps to reduce risks of heart disease, stroke and cancer.

AVOCADO AND SMOKED SALMON
with sunflower seed salad

Preparation time: 10 minutes

Serves 2

2 slices smoked salmon, about 100 g
(3½ oz) each

1 small, firm avocado, sliced into wedges

juice of ½ lime

2 teaspoons reduced-calorie mayonnaise

1 teaspoon wholegrain mustard

2 tablespoons chopped dill

TO SERVE

25 g (1 oz) rocket leaves

2 teaspoons sunflower seeds

CARBOHYDRATE 3 g

FAT 20 g

PROTEIN 29 g

ENERGY 305 kcal/1270 kJ

1 Wrap the smoked salmon slices around the sliced avocado and sprinkle with lime juice.

2 Mix the mayonnaise with the mustard and dill.

3 Serve the wrapped avocado on a bed of rocket leaves with the mustard mayonnaise. Sprinkle with sunflower seeds.

Nutrition note

Avocado, although rich in fat, contains the more beneficial type of mono-unsaturated fat.

THAI CHICKEN SALAD
with basil and peanut dressing

Preparation time: 10 minutes

Cooking time: 15–20 minutes

Serves 4

150 g (5 oz) cooked chicken breast, shredded

3 tablespoons coriander leaves

150 g (5 oz) pak choi, shredded

DRESSING

1 tablespoon groundnut oil

1 tablespoon Thai fish sauce

juice of 1 lime

juice of 1 small orange

1 garlic clove, crushed

3 tablespoons roughly chopped basil leaves

30 g (1¼ oz) unsalted peanuts, skins removed and chopped

black pepper

TO GARNISH

2 spring onions, green stems only, shredded lengthways

1 plump red chilli, deseeded and sliced diagonally

CARBOHYDRATE 4 g

FAT 7 g

PROTEIN 16 g

ENERGY 144 kcal/604 kJ

1 Make the dressing by shaking all the ingredients together in a screw-top jar.

2 Mix the chicken with the coriander leaves and stir in the dressing.

3 Line a serving dish with the pak choi, spoon the dressed chicken on top and serve chilled, garnished with spring onion shreds and red chilli slices.

Nutrition notes

Chicken breast is one of the lowest fat meats.

Peanuts add valuable mono-unsaturated fat, vitamin E and a range of important minerals to this recipe. A handful of peanuts as part of a balanced diet can help reduce blood cholesterol levels and help you manage your weight.

GRIDDLED AUBERGINES
with chilli toasts

Preparation time: 15 minutes

Cooking time: 10 minutes

Serves 4

2 aubergines, about 550 g (1lb 2 oz) in total

2 teaspoons olive oil

50 g (2 oz) sun-blush tomatoes

2 garlic cloves, crushed

4 tablespoons lemon juice

CHILLI TOASTS

4 slices multigrain bread

1 tablespoon chilli-infused oil

TO GARNISH

4 basil leaves

black pepper

CARBOHYDRATE 15 g

FAT 6 g

PROTEIN 4 g

ENERGY 122 kcal/513 kJ

1 Prepare the chilli toasts. Remove the crusts from each slice of bread and cut the remaining bread into two neat triangles. Brush each side of the bread with the chilli-infused oil and put the bread on an ovenproof baking sheet.

2 Cut the aubergines lengthways into 5 mm (¼ inch) slices and season with black pepper.

3 Put the chilli toasts in a preheated oven, 220°C (425°F), Gas Mark 7, and cook for 8–10 minutes until crisp and golden.

4 Meanwhile, oil a ridged griddle pan and heat it. Put the aubergine slices and sun-blush tomatoes on the pan with the garlic and cook for about 4 minutes until they start to soften. Turn over the aubergines and cook for a further 4 minutes. Finally, add the lemon juice.

5 Remove the chilli toasts from the oven and serve with the aubergine and tomato piled high in the centre of each plate and garnished with basil leaves and black pepper.

Nutrition notes

These Mediterranean vegetables are full of great antioxidants, which will help your body's immune system.

Multigrain breads have a lower GI than either wholemeal or white bread.

Fantastic
Fish

SCALLOPS IN PANCETTA
on lemon lentils

Preparation time: 15 minutes

Cooking time: 45 minutes

Serves 4

16 scallops, about 400 g (13 oz) in total,
roe removed

2 tablespoons chopped oregano leaves

200 g (7 oz) pancetta, cut into 16 thin slices

LEMON LENTILS

1 teaspoon olive oil

1 onion, chopped

6 cloves

225 g (7½ oz) Puy lentils, washed

400 ml (14 fl oz) Vegetable Stock (see page 14)

400 ml (14 fl oz) hot water

⅛ teaspoon asafoetida

4–6 tablespoons lemon juice

black pepper

TO GARNISH

mixed salad leaves

1 lemon, cut into 4 wedges

150 g (5 oz) reduced-fat Greek yogurt
sprinkled with lemon zest

handful of oregano leaves

CARBOHYDRATE 36 g

FAT 16 g

PROTEIN 47 g

ENERGY 467 kcal/1967 kJ

1 Prepare the lemon lentils by heating the olive oil in a saucepan over medium to low heat. Add the onion and cook for about 5 minutes, stirring occasionally, until it begins to brown. Add the whole cloves and lentils and cook for 5 minutes.

2 Pour in the vegetable stock, the measurement water and the asafoetida and bring to the boil. Simmer gently, uncovered, for 30 minutes until the lentils are tender.

3 Meanwhile, sprinkle the scallops with the chopped oregano and wrap each in a slice of pancetta. Thread 4 scallop parcels on to a skewer. Repeat with the remaining scallops. Grill the scallops on a barbecue or under a preheated hot grill for 2–3 minutes each side until they are golden-brown.

4 Remove and discard the cloves from the lentils and stir in the lemon juice and black pepper. Serve garnished with mixed salad leaves, a lemon wedge and yogurt, and sprinkled with oregano leaves.

Nutrition note

Lentils are packed with soluble fibre and are valuable for keeping blood sugar levels evenly balanced. They also help to keep the GI content of the meal down as well as providing a tasty, filling alternative to rice.

LEMON SOLE
with butter and dill

Preparation time: 10 minutes

Cooking time: 10–15 minutes

Serves 4

4 sweet potatoes, about 750 g (1½ lb) in total, sliced

1 tablespoon olive oil

2 tablespoons plain flour

30 g (1¼ oz) dill, chopped

4 lemon sole fillets, about 600 g (1¼ lb) in total

50 g (2 oz) butter

4 tablespoons lemon juice

salt and black pepper

CARBOHYDRATE 49 g

FAT 16 g

PROTEIN 29 g

ENERGY 443 kcal/1868 kJ

1 Boil the sweet potatoes in lightly salted water for about 5 minutes until just tender. Drain, drizzle with the olive oil and keep warm.

2 Mix together the flour and dill with some seasoning. Coat each fillet with this seasoned flour.

3 Heat the butter in a large frying pan and pan-fry the fish for about 3 minutes on each side.

4 Serve the fish, drizzled with lemon juice, on the still warm sliced sweet potatoes.

Nutrition note

Sweet potatoes are a good source of the antioxidant vitamin betacarotene, and they have a lower GI rating than standard potatoes.

BAKED TROUT FILLET
with toasted pine nuts

Preparation time: 5 minutes
Cooking time: 15–20 minutes
Serves 4

1 trout fillet, about 600 g (1¼ lb)
15 g (½ oz) dill, roughly chopped
3 spring onions, sliced
1–2 teaspoons lemon pepper
10 g (½ oz) pine nuts
salt
mixed salad leaves, to serve
1 orange, peeled, pith removed and sliced, to garnish

CARBOHYDRATE 4 g
FAT 10 g
PROTEIN 3 g
ENERGY 222 kcal/935 kJ

1 Place the trout fillet, skin side down, on a foil-lined baking sheet. Sprinkle the dill, spring onions, lemon pepper and salt over the trout and cover tightly with foil.

2 Bake the trout in a preheated oven, 200°C (400°F), Gas Mark 6, for 15–20 minutes.

3 Meanwhile, toast the pine nuts in a heavy-based frying pan for 1–2 minutes.

4 Sprinkle the toasted pine nuts over the trout and serve on a bed of mixed salad leaves, garnished with slices of orange.

Nutrition note
Trout is rich in natural omega-3 fatty acids, which are known to protect the heart. Because it is an oily fish, there is no need to add extra fat for cooking.

PAN-FRIED HALIBUT
with papaya and coriander salsa

Preparation time: 20 minutes

Cooking time: 10–12 minutes

Serves 4

2 teaspoons olive oil

3 garlic cloves, crushed

4 halibut steaks, about 600 g (1¼ lb) in total

salt and black pepper

watercress leaves, to serve

SALSA

1 papaya, cut into cubes

½ red onion, finely chopped

15 g (½ oz) coriander leaves, finely chopped

¼–½ teaspoon red chilli powder

1 red pepper, cored, deseeded and finely chopped

juice of ½ lime

CARBOHYDRATE 20 g

FAT 6 g

PROTEIN 28 g

ENERGY 236 kcal/993 kJ

1 Heat the oil in a large, nonstick frying pan. Add the garlic and stir for a few seconds. Put the fish steaks in the pan and fry for 10–12 minutes until just cooked, turning halfway through cooking.

2 Meanwhile, make the salsa by mixing together all the ingredients.

3 Serve the halibut steaks on a bed of watercress leaves, with the salsa and lime wedges on the side.

Nutrition notes

Using salmon instead of halibut in this recipe will boost your intake of omega-3 fat.

The chunky papaya and peppers, together with the acidic lime, help to lower the glycaemic index of any other carbohydrates that you may be serving to accompany this dish.

MONKFISH TERIYAKI

Preparation time: 15 minutes

Cooking time: 15–20 minutes

Serves 4

2 garlic cloves, crushed

2 cm (¾ inch) fresh ginger root, peeled and shredded

2 dessertspoons reduced-salt soy sauce

½ teaspoon rice wine vinegar

600 g (1¼ lb) monkfish tail, bones removed and cubed

1 tablespoon chopped chives, to garnish

ROASTED ASPARAGUS

200 g (7 oz) asparagus tips

1 tablespoon olive oil

BEAN SPROUT SALAD

200 g (7 oz) bean sprouts

60 g (2½ oz) hot pickled pimento peppers, drained and finely sliced

CARBOHYDRATE 5 g

FAT 4 g

PROTEIN 28 g

ENERGY 162 kcal/682 kJ

1 Mix together the crushed garlic, ginger, soy sauce and rice vinegar.

2 Put the monkfish cubes in a non-metallic ovenproof dish and pour over the soy sauce mixture. Cover with a lid.

3 Arrange the asparagus tips in a shallow roasting tin and spoon over the olive oil. Shake to coat but do not cover.

4 Roast both the fish and the asparagus in a preheated oven, 200°C (400°F), Gas Mark 6, for 15–20 minutes.

5 Meanwhile, mix the bean sprouts with the pimento peppers.

6 Arrange the bean sprout salad in the centre of the plates and top with the monkfish. Pour over the hot fishy juices and garnish with chopped chives. Serve with the roasted asparagus.

Nutrition notes

White fish contains little fat and should be roasted in liquid to keep it moist.

Using reduced-salt soy sauce imparts a wonderful flavour and helps avoid overdoing the salt, which has been linked with high blood pressure.

CARIBBEAN MACKEREL
with avocado salsa

Preparation time: 30 minutes, plus marinating

Cooking time: 5 minutes

Serves 4

4 mackerel fillets, about 750 g (1½ lb) in total

juice of 6 limes

100 ml (3½ fl oz) dark rum

1 lime, sliced, to garnish

AVOCADO SALSA

275 g (9 oz) tomatoes

1 medium avocado, finely chopped

½ small red onion, finely chopped

1 tablespoon chopped coriander

juice of 1 lime

a few drops of Tabasco sauce

CARBOHYDRATE 5 g

FAT 39 g

PROTEIN 37 g

ENERGY 577 kcal/2394 kJ

1 Make 2–3 small slashes in the flesh of the mackerel so that the marinade will penetrate. Place the fish in a shallow dish.

2 Mix together the rum and lime juice and pour it over the mackerel. Place the mackerel in the refrigerator for 2–3 hours, removing it and turning it in the marinade every 30 minutes.

3 Make the salsa. Skin the tomatoes by cutting a cross in the bottom of each one. Pour boiling water over them and leave for 1 minute before draining and slipping off the skins when they are cool enough to handle. Cut each tomato in half and, holding it cut side down over a plate, squeeze gently to extract the seeds. Chop the tomato flesh as finely as possible.

4 Combine the tomatoes and avocado with the onion and coriander in a bowl with the lime juice and Tabasco. Cover and leave for at least 1 hour for the flavours to mingle and develop.

5 Remove the mackerel from the marinade and cook under a preheated hot grill for 5 minutes. Serve accompanied by the avocado salsa and garnished with sliced lime.

Nutrition note
Avocado and oily fish are both rich in fat, but the good news is that this is healthier, mono-unsaturated, fat. Both foods also contain a wealth of vitamins.

CHUNKY MUSSEL SOUP

Preparation time: 35 minutes

Cooking time: about 45 minutes

Serves 4

1 tablespoon olive oil

175 g (6 oz) shallots, sliced

1 garlic clove, finely chopped

2 bay leaves

1 kg (2 lb) mussels in their shells, prepared (see note below)

1 tablespoon chopped tarragon

1 tablespoon chopped thyme

1 tablespoon chopped oregano

a good pinch of saffron

125 g (4 oz) bean sprouts

50 g (2 oz) baby spinach leaves

200 g (7 oz) reduced-fat Greek yogurt

FISH STOCK

1.5 kg (3 lb) fish trimmings (from any fish except oily fish)

1 onion, sliced

1 small leek, white part only, sliced

1 celery stick, chopped

1 bay leaf

6 parsley stalks

10 whole peppercorns

475 ml (16 fl oz) dry white wine

1.8 litres (3 pints) water

TO SERVE

2 tablespoons chopped parsley

8 slices sourdough bread

CARBOHYDRATE 26 g

FAT 7 g

PROTEIN 20 g

ENERGY 239 kcal/1010 kJ

1 Make the fish stock. Put all the ingredients in a large saucepan. Bring slowly to just below boiling point and simmer gently for 20 minutes, removing any scum that rises to the surface. Strain the stock through a muslin-lined sieve, return to the pan and keep warm. The ingredients above will make about 1.8 litres (3 pints), and any stock not used can be chilled then frozen for use in other dishes.

2 Meanwhile, heat the oil in a large, deep pan and add the shallots, garlic and bay leaves. Cover and cook for 6 minutes to soften.

3 Put the mussels in the pan and add 900 ml (1½ pints) of the hot fish stock. Bring to the boil, cover and cook on a fairly high heat, shaking the pan occasionally, for 3 minutes until the mussels have opened. Discard any mussels that are still closed.

4 Use a slotted spoon to transfer half the mussels in their shells to large, shallow soup bowls. Keep warm. Remove the remainder of the mussels from their shells and add them to the soup bowls.

5 Add the herbs, saffron, bean sprouts and spinach to the stock remaining in the pan. Boil for 3 minutes, reduce the heat and stir in the yogurt.

6 Discard the bay leaves and ladle the stock over the mussels. Sprinkle with chopped parsley and serve with sourdough bread to soak up the liquid.

Preparing mussels Scrub the mussels under cold, running water and pull or scrape off any tufts of hair (known as the beard) that protrude from the shell. Tap any mussels that are slightly open with the back of a knife and discard them if they do not close. Also discard any mussels that float in liquid or have broken shells. Make sure that you discard any mussels that have not opened after cooking.

JAPANESE-STYLE SALMON STEAKS

Preparation time: 5 minutes, plus marinating

Cooking time: 10 minutes

Serves 4

4 salmon fillets, about 750 g (1½ lb) in total

125 g (4 oz) dried flat rice noodles

2 tablespoons sesame oil

4 star anise

4 spring onions, green stems only, sliced thinly lengthways, to garnish

MARINADE

50 ml (2 fl oz) Japanese soy sauce

½ teaspoon wasabi paste

4 tablespoons teriyaki sauce

4 tablespoons rice wine vinegar

2.5 cm (1 inch) fresh root ginger, peeled and shredded

1 teaspoon black pepper

CARBOHYDRATE 27 g

FAT 28 g

PROTEIN 37 g

ENERGY 514 kcal/2140 kJ

1 Make the marinade. Mix together all the ingredients and use the mixture to coat the fish. Set aside for at least 20 minutes.

2 Cook the noodles in lightly salted boiling water for 2–3 minutes or according to packet instructions.

3 Heat 1 tablespoon of the sesame oil in a heavy-based, nonstick frying pan and fry the star anise to release the aroma for a few seconds.

4 Carefully place the salmon, skin side down, in the pan, adding any remaining marinade juices. Fry gently on each side for 3–4 minutes.

5 Meanwhile, heat the remaining oil and stir in the noodles to heat them through.

6 Serve the salmon on a bed of noodles, garnished with crisscross strips of spring onion.

Nutrition note

Salmon is an oil-rich fish, and you should aim to eat oily fish once a week.

SEARED TUNA
with lemon salsa

Preparation time: 30 minutes, plus marinating

Cooking time: 5 minutes

Serves 4

4 tuna steaks, about 400 g (13 oz) in total, cut about 1.5 cm (¾ inch) thick

3 garlic cloves, finely chopped

1 teaspoon fennel seeds, finely ground with a pestle and mortar

2 small dried red chillies, crumbled

1 tablespoon olive oil

4 tablespoons lemon juice

LEMON SALSA

250 g (8 oz) beef tomatoes, skinned, seeds removed (see page 43) and finely chopped

1 small red onion, finely chopped

1 garlic clove, crushed

½ green chilli, deseeded and chopped

2 tablespoons lemon juice

grated rind from 1 unwaxed lemon

25 g (1 oz) coriander leaves, chopped

a pinch of caster sugar

TO GARNISH

grated rind from 1 unwaxed lemon

a handful of watercress leaves

CARBOHYDRATE 5 g

FAT 8 g

PROTEIN 25 g

ENERGY 190 kcal/799 kJ

1 Place the tuna steaks on a chopping board and rub half the garlic into one side of the steaks, followed by half the ground fennel seeds and one of the chillies. Turn the steaks over and repeat the process on the other side with the remaining garlic, fennel and chilli.

2 Place the fish in a shallow container and pour over the olive oil and lemon juice. Cover and leave to marinate for 1 hour.

3 Meanwhile, make the lemon salsa. Combine all the ingredients together in a bowl and put to one side to let the flavours develop.

4 Preheat a griddle or barbecue grill to very hot and sear the tuna for 1–2 minutes on each side. The tuna should be pink in the middle when it is served. If you prefer it cooked through, cook for an additional 2 minutes on each side.

5 Serve the tuna hot with the lemon salsa and garnished with watercress leaves and the lemon rind.

BUTTERFLY PRAWNS
with courgette ribbons

Preparation time: 30 minutes, plus marinating

Cooking time: 5 minutes

Serves 4

450 g (14½ oz) courgettes, topped and tailed and sliced into fine ribbons with a vegetable peeler

28 raw peeled large prawns with tails still intact, heads removed

a handful of chopped flat leaf parsley, to garnish

MARINADE

a large pinch of saffron threads

8 tablespoons lemon juice

6 garlic cloves, roughly chopped

2 tablespoons rice wine vinegar

4 tablespoons olive oil

2 tablespoons drained capers

CARBOHYDRATE 6 g

FAT 12 g

PROTEIN 12 g

ENERGY 175 kcal/728 kJ

1 Make the marinade. Mix together all the marinade ingredients, lightly crushing the capers against the side of the bowl.

2 Place the courgette ribbons in a large bowl and spoon two-thirds of the marinade mixture on top. Marinate for 3–4 hours.

3 Prepare the prawns. Hold the tail underside up and cut each prawn in half lengthways. Pull out any black intestinal thread, rinse, pat dry on kitchen paper and put in a shallow dish. Alternatively, ask your fishmonger to prepare the prawns for you. Pour the remaining marinade over the prawns and marinate for 3–4 hours.

4 Place the courgettes in a large frying pan with their marinade and simmer over a medium-low heat for 3–5 minutes.

5 Grill the prawns for 3–4 minutes until pink and sizzling, basting with the marinade. Be careful not to overcook them.

6 To serve, pile the courgettes in the centre of a warmed dish, top with the prawns and garnish with chopped parsley.

Nutrition notes

These delicious courgettes are an elegant substitute for pasta and help lower the GI content of the meal.

Prawns do contain cholesterol, but it is saturated fat that is more likely to raise your blood cholesterol rather than the cholesterol that is found in prawns.

PLAICE EN PAPILLOTTE
with fennel and chilli

Preparation time: 30 minutes

Cooking time: 10 minutes

Serves 4

1 fennel bulb, about 360 g (11½ oz)

2 red chillies, deseeded and chopped

4 tablespoons lemon juice

2 teaspoons extra virgin olive oil

4 plaice fillets, about 650 g (1 lb 6 oz) in total

1 small handful chopped dill

½ lemon, cut into wedges, to garnish

RADICCHIO AND ORANGE SALAD

200 g (7 oz) red radicchio leaves

2 large oranges, peeled and pith removed, separated into segments

CARBOHYDRATE 13 g

FAT 6 g

PROTEIN 32 g

ENERGY 234 kcal/988 kJ

1 Finely chop the fennel bulb and put it in a bowl with the chopped chillies. Add the lemon juice and olive oil and set aside.

2 Cut 4 sheets of baking parchment, each 35 x 18 cm (14 x 7 inches), and fold them in half widthways. Lay one half of a sheet over a plate and arrange a fish fillet on one side of the fold. Sprinkle over some chopped dill and fold over the paper to enclose the filling. Fold in the edges and pleat to secure. Repeat with the remaining fish.

3 Place the wrapped fish on a baking sheet and cook in a preheated oven, 220°C (425°F), Gas Mark 7, for about 8 minutes or until the paper is puffed up and brown.

4 Make the salad. Combine the radicchio with the orange segments.

5 Place each fish parcel on a large plate and cut an X-shaped slit in the top, or pull the paper apart to open the parcel, releasing a fragrant puff of steam, and curl back the paper. Serve with individual side bowls of the fennel and chilli mixture and radicchio and orange salad, and garnish with a lemon wedge.

Nutrition notes

Fresh fish is very low in fat.

Oranges are a good source of vitamin C, an important antioxidant vitamin.

Mouthwatering Meat

ROSEMARY LAMB SHANKS

with red onions and spiced beans

Preparation time: 10 minutes, plus marinating

Cooking time: 2–2½ hours

Serves 4

4 lamb shanks, about 1.25 kg (2½ lb) in total, fat removed

4–5 rosemary sprigs

2 garlic cloves, thinly sliced

4 small red onions, halved

3 tablespoons balsamic vinegar

MARINADE

small bunch of thyme, leaves removed from stalks

3 whole cardamom pods

1 bay leaf

a pinch of saffron threads

4 tablespoons lemon juice

salt and black pepper

SPICED BEANS

2 teaspoons rapeseed oil

½ teaspoon black mustard seeds

½ teaspoon onion seeds

1 tablespoon tomato purée

pinch of ground turmeric

¼–½ teaspoon red chilli powder

2 x 300 g (10 oz) cans pinto beans, drained

2 tablespoons chopped coriander leaves, plus extra to serve

CARBOHYDRATE 10 g

FAT 14 g

PROTEIN 33 g

ENERGY 293 kcal/1230 kJ

1 Place the lamb shanks in a large roasting tin, make slits in each shank and insert sprigs of rosemary and slices of garlic inside.

2 Make the marinade. Mix all the ingredients together. Coat the lamb shanks with the marinade, cover with foil and put in the refrigerator for at least 1 hour.

3 Cook the lamb in a preheated oven, 160°C (325°F), Gas Mark 3, for 2–2½ hours, basting every 45 minutes or so, until the meat is tender.

4 Meanwhile, prepare the beans. Heat the oil and cook the mustard and onion seeds over a low heat, allowing them to pop for a few seconds. Stir in the tomato purée, turmeric and chilli powder and mix well. Add the beans, stir well and add a few tablespoons of hot water. Cover and allow to cook for a few minutes. Stir in the chopped coriander leaves and remove from the heat.

5 Preheat the grill. Place the halved onions, cut sides up, in a heatproof dish, pour over the vinegar and cook under a preheated medium grill for about 20 minutes until they are soft.

6 Serve the lamb accompanied by the spiced beans and grilled red onions and sprinkled with chopped coriander leaves.

Nutrition note

Lean lamb is a good source of zinc and also of iron, which is available in a form that is readily absorbed.

LAMB SHANKS
with roasted new potatoes

Preparation time: 20 minutes, plus resting

Cooking time: 3 hours

Serves 4

4 lamb shanks, about 300 g (10 oz) each

6–8 tablespoons lemon juice

¼ teaspoon dried oregano

¼ teaspoon dried thyme

2 oregano sprigs

4 lemon thyme sprigs

salt and black pepper

ROASTED NEW POTATOES

500 g (1 lb) small new potatoes, skins left on

2 teaspoons olive oil

2 oregano sprigs

4 lemon thyme sprigs

2 bay leaves

2 large beef tomatoes, about 500 g (1 lb) in total, thickly sliced

CARBOHYDRATE 24 g

FAT 14 g

PROTEIN 32 g

ENERGY 347 kcal/1460 kJ

1 Put 2 large sheets of foil crossways in a roasting tin. These will make a large sealed envelope to steam the meat in its own juices.

2 Remove any skin and excess fat from the lamb shanks and place them in the lined roasting tin. Sprinkle the lemon juice, dried herbs, salt and some black pepper evenly over the meat. Tear the leaves from the oregano and thyme sprigs and put them around the meat.

3 Fold over the foil to form a sealed parcel and cook in a preheated oven, 180°C (350°F), Gas Mark 4, for 3 hours.

4 Put the new potatoes in a flat roasting dish and roll them in the olive oil to coat. Tear the leaves from the oregano and thyme sprigs and lay the slices of beef tomatoes over the top. One hour from the end of the cooking time for the meat, put the potatoes and tomatoes, uncovered, in the oven.

5 When the meat is cooked remove it from the oven and leave it to rest for 10 minutes. Remove the bay leaves from the caramelized potatoes and tomatoes before serving alongside the lamb shanks, drizzled with any remaining cooking juices.

Nutrition note
New potatoes are lower in GI than many other types of potato, and leaving the skins on provides extra fibre.

EXOTIC LAMB BROCHETTES

Preparation time: 15 minutes, plus marinating

Cooking time: 5–10 minutes

Serves 4

500 g (1 lb) lamb fillet, cut into small cubes

juice of 2 kiwifruit

16 chestnut mushrooms

16 oyster mushrooms

1 teaspoon olive oil

4 garlic cloves, crushed

1 tablespoon finely chopped rosemary

TO SERVE

1 lemon, cut into wedges

8 pitta breads, warmed

mixed salad leaves

CARBOHYDRATE 45 g

FAT 13 g

PROTEIN 34 g

ENERGY 423 kcal/1785 kJ

1 Put the lamb cubes in a shallow dish, pour the kiwifruit juice over the meat and marinate for 2–3 hours.

2 Brush the mushrooms with the oil. Thread the marinated lamb cubes on to 8 skewers, alternating with the two different types of mushroom. Scatter the crushed garlic and chopped rosemary over the brochettes.

3 Cook under a preheated hot grill or on a barbecue for 5–10 minutes, turning occasionally so that the brochettes cook evenly.

4 Serve with lemon wedges, warmed pitta breads and mixed salad leaves.

Nutrition notes

Mushrooms, particularly oriental types, contain compounds that are reputed to stimulate the immune system and may help to reduce blood cholesterol levels.

Pitta bread has a more favourable GI than white bread or baguette.

LAMB NOISETTES
with herb crust on tangy butter beans

Preparation time: 10 minutes
Cooking time: 15–20 minutes
Serves 4

2 tablespoons finely chopped mint
1 tablespoon finely chopped thyme
1 tablespoon finely chopped oregano
½ tablespoon finely chopped rosemary
4 teaspoons wholegrain mustard
4 lamb noisettes, about 125 g (4 oz) each
mixed salad leaves, to serve (optional)

TANGY BUTTER BEANS
2 teaspoons vegetable oil
1 medium onion, chopped
1 tablespoon tomato purée
50 ml (2 fl oz) pineapple juice
2 tablespoons lemon juice
a few drops of Tabasco sauce
black pepper
250 g (8 oz) cooked butter beans or drained canned beans

CARBOHYDRATE 14 g
FAT 14 g
PROTEIN 32 g
ENERGY 305 kcal/1280 kJ

1 Mix together all the chopped herbs in a bowl. Spread mustard on both sides of each noisette and dip the meat into the herb mixture. Press the herbs firmly to the mustard. Chill the lamb in the refrigerator until you are ready to cook.

2 Make the tangy butter beans. Heat the oil in a frying pan and fry the onion until it has softened. Add the rest of the ingredients to the frying pan and cook gently for 5 minutes.

3 Preheat the grill to hot and cook the lamb noisettes for about 4 minutes each side. The lamb should be cooked but still retain a slight pink colour.

4 Serve the lamb immediately surrounded by the tangy butter beans and accompanied by mixed salad leaves, if liked.

Nutrition notes
The delicious butter beans that replace potato in this recipe keep the GI of the meal low.

Serve some lightly steamed green vegetables with the meal to lower the GI even further.

CHERMOULA CHICKEN

Preparation time: 45 minutes, plus marinating

Cooking time: 1 hour

Serves 4

1kg (2 lb) chicken pieces on the bone (such as thighs, legs or quarters), skin removed

chopped parsley, to garnish

SPICE MIX

1 large onion, finely chopped

2 large garlic cloves, finely chopped

½ teaspoon ground cumin

¼ teaspoon paprika

¼–½ teaspoon crushed dried chillies

1–2 pinches of saffron threads

6 tablespoons finely chopped coriander

6 tablespoons finely chopped flat leaf parsley

2 tablespoons olive oil

2 tablespoons lemon juice

PEARL BARLEY

1 teaspoon vegetable oil

1 small onion, chopped

200 g (7 oz) pearl barley, washed

900 ml (1½ pints) hot Chicken Stock (see page 69)

RAITA

150 g (5 oz) reduced-fat natural yogurt

125 g (4 oz) cucumber, grated

pinch of ground cumin

CARBOHYDRATE 52 g

FAT 13 g

PROTEIN 30 g

ENERGY 428 kcal/1800 kJ

1 Combine all the ingredients for the spice mix in a bowl. Rub the spice mix all over the chicken flesh. Set the chicken aside for at least 2 hours to absorb the flavours.

2 Prepare the pearl barley. Heat the oil in a large, heavy-based frying pan and cook the onion gently until soft, stirring so it does not brown. Add the washed barley and cook for 2 minutes. Pour in the hot stock and simmer for 1 hour, stirring occasionally, until all the fluid has been absorbed and the grains are soft.

3 Meanwhile, cook the chicken, uncovered, in a preheated oven, 190°C (375°F), Gas Mark 5, for 30–40 minutes until it is tender throughout.

4 Make the raita. Combine the yogurt and grated cucumber and sprinkle some cumin on the top.

5 When the chicken and pearl barley are cooked, garnish the chicken with chopped parsley and serve immediately with the pearl barley and raita.

Nutrition notes

Removing the skin from the chicken not only reduces the fat content considerably but also has the advantage of allowing the spice flavours to penetrate the chicken flesh.

Pearl barley is often overlooked in cooking, yet it has a low GI of only 25 and is high in soluble fibre.

MOROCCAN LAMB AND PRUNE TAGINE

Preparation time: 35 minutes, plus marinating

Cooking time: 5¼–5¾ hours

Serves 4

500 ml (17 fl oz) Beef Stock (see page 74)

750 g (1½ lb) leg of lamb, fat removed, cubed

1 tablespoon olive oil

1 large onion, finely chopped

350 g (11½ oz) tomatoes, chopped

125 g (4 oz) ready-to-eat prunes

25 g (1 oz) whole almonds, roughly chopped

½ teaspoon saffron threads

30 g (1¼ oz) flat leaf parsley, chopped

30 g (1¼ oz) coriander leaves, chopped

couscous, to serve (optional)

MARINADE

½ teaspoon crushed ginger

2 garlic cloves, crushed

½–1 teaspoon black pepper

1 teaspoon ground cinnamon

1 teaspoon ground turmeric

3 teaspoons paprika

1 teaspoon red chilli powder

TO GARNISH

15 g (½ oz) coriander leaves, finely chopped

1 tablespoon flaked almonds

CARBOHYDRATE 19 g

FAT 16 g

PROTEIN 25 g

ENERGY 320 kcal/1340 kJ

1 Make the beef stock. When the stock has simmered for 2½ hours or so, make the marinade by mixing together all the ingredients. Add the cubed lamb and mix well. Leave the meat to marinate for 1 hour, or longer, if liked.

2 Heat the oil in a large, heavy-based pan with a lid. Add the lamb with the marinade and brown over a medium heat. Stir in the onion and cook for about 5 minutes. Add the tomatoes and the hot beef stock and cook gently for 5–10 minutes.

3 Stir in the remaining ingredients, cover and simmer, stirring occasionally, for 1–1½ hours until the lamb is tender and the liquid has reduced.

4 Garnish with coriander, spring onions and flaked almonds and serve with couscous, if liked.

Nutrition note

Prunes add valuable fibre to this delicious and exotic dish.

PAN-FRIED CHICKEN LIVERS
with fennel

Preparation time: 5 minutes

Cooking time: 10–12 minutes

Serves 4

1 tablespoon plain flour

225 g (7½ oz) chicken livers

2 teaspoons olive oil

225 g (7½ oz) fennel bulb and leaves, sliced

3 tablespoons chopped flat leaf parsley

2 tablespoons lemon juice

salt and black pepper

watercress leaves, to serve

CARBOHYDRATE 6 g

FAT 5 g

PROTEIN 12 g

ENERGY 115 kcal/483 kJ

1 Mix the flour with a little salt and black pepper and use the seasoned flour to coat the chicken livers.

2 Heat the oil in a large frying pan and stir-fry the fennel over a moderately high heat for 3 minutes.

3 Add the seasoned liver to the pan and cook, stirring gently, over a high heat for 5–8 minutes.

4 Slowly mix in the parsley. Pour in the lemon juice, which will make a sizzling sound, remove from the heat and serve on a bed of watercress leaves.

Nutrition note

Liver is rich in iron and vitamin B12, a vitamin that plays an essential role in the body's ability to produce red blood cells.

GINGER-SPICED TURKEY ESCALOPES
with cashew nut chutney

Preparation time: 8 minutes

Cooking times: 12–15 minutes

Serves 4

2 tablespoons plain flour

1 teaspoon crushed ginger

1 teaspoon finely chopped tarragon

1 teaspoon dried mixed herbs

4 skinless turkey breasts, about 175 g (6 oz) each

1 tablespoon corn or rapeseed oil

salt and black pepper

CASHEW NUT CHUTNEY

60 g (2½ oz) unsalted cashew nuts, coarsely ground

15 g (½ oz) basil leaves, chopped

1 red onion, finely diced

½ teaspoon red chilli powder

½ teaspoon curry powder

juice of 1 lime

juice of 1 orange

black pepper

CARBOHYDRATE 13 g

FAT 14 g

PROTEIN 42 g

ENERGY 344 kcal/1447 kJ

1 Mix the flour with the ginger, tarragon and mixed herbs and season with salt and black pepper. Use this mixture to coat both sides of each turkey breast.

2 Heat the oil in a nonstick ridged griddle pan. Cook the turkey over a medium heat for 12–15 minutes until fully cooked, turning once only to achieve a decorative ridged effect.

3 Meanwhile, make the cashew nut chutney by mixing together all the ingredients.

4 Serve the turkey breasts immediately accompanied by the cashew nut chutney.

Nutrition notes

Turkey meat is naturally low in fat.

Cashew nuts are rich in fat, but remember that this is the healthy mono-unsaturated type

SERIOUSLY HOT JERK CHICKEN

with sweet potato wedges

Preparation time: 20 minutes

Cooking time: 50 minutes

Serves 4

4 skinless chicken breast fillets, about 500 g (1 lb) in total

JERK SEASONING

8–10 allspice berries

2 spring onions, green part only, sliced

4 garlic cloves, crushed

1 cm (½ inch) fresh root ginger, peeled and shredded

pinch of finely grated nutmeg

2 pinches of ground cinnamon

1 teaspoon thyme leaves

1–2 Scotch Bonnet chillies, deseeded and finely chopped

2 tablespoons reduced-salt soy sauce

juice of 2 limes

SWEET POTATO WEDGES

2 orange-fleshed sweet potatoes, about 750 g (1½ lb) in total, unpeeled

1 tablespoon olive oil

2 tablespoons chopped parsley

2 tablespoons chopped chives

CARBOHYDRATE 40 g

FAT 7 g

PROTEIN 31 g

ENERGY 343 kcal/1452 kJ

1 Make the jerk seasoning. Crush the allspice berries using a pestle and mortar or a blender. Add the spring onions and pound until well mixed. Add the garlic, ginger, nutmeg, cinnamon, thyme leaves and chillies. Stir in the soy sauce and lime juice and mix well. If necessary, add a little water to bind.

2 Score the chicken breasts on both sides and rub in the seasoning. Bake the chicken in a preheated oven, 190°C (375°F), Gas Mark 5, for 30–40 minutes until it is crusty on the outside.

3 Meanwhile, put the sweet potatoes in cold water and bring to the boil. Cook the potatoes for 8–10 minutes until parboiled, drain and leave to cool. Remove the skins and cut into wedges.

4 Heat the oil in a nonstick frying pan and fry the wedges for about 10 minutes until they are coloured on both sides. Sprinkle with the parsley and chives and serve with the cooked chicken cut into thick slices.

Nutrition note
To remove excess fat from the sweet potato wedges, pat them dry on kitchen paper before sprinkling with the fresh herbs.

PEANUT AND CHICKEN CASSOULET

Preparation time: 35–40 minutes

Cooking time: 3½ hours

Serves 4

1 teaspoon vegetable oil

1 onion, chopped

1 garlic clove, crushed

1 green pepper, cored, deseeded and diced

500 g (1 lb) chicken breast fillets, each fillet divided into 3 small pieces or fingers

75 g (3 oz) peanut butter

60 g (2½ oz) unsalted peanuts, skins removed and crushed

1 tablespoon ground coriander

1 teaspoon ground cumin

1 teaspoon red chilli powder

2 tomatoes, roughly chopped

250 g (8 oz) cooked or canned and drained chickpeas

2 tablespoons chopped coriander leaves, to garnish

CHICKEN STOCK

1 cooked chicken carcass

raw giblets and trimmings (optional)

1 onion, chopped

2–3 carrots, chopped

1 celery stick, chopped

1 bay leaf

3–4 parsley stalks

1 thyme sprig

1.8 litres (3 pints) water

CARBOHYDRATE 20 g

FAT 24 g

PROTEIN 41 g

ENERGY 460 kcal/1920 kJ

1 Make the chicken stock. Chop the chicken carcass into 3–4 pieces and put them in a large saucepan with the rest of the ingredients. Bring to the boil, removing any scum that rises to the surface. Lower the heat and simmer for 2–2½ hours. Strain the stock through a muslin-lined sieve, return to the saucepan and keep warm. These ingredients will make about 1 litre (1¾ pints), and any stock not used in this recipe can be chilled then frozen for use in other dishes.

2 Meanwhile, using an ovenproof casserole dish that can go on the hob, heat the oil and fry the onion, garlic and green pepper for 5 minutes until soft. Add the chicken pieces and allow to colour for 5 minutes.

3 Mix the peanut butter, crushed peanuts, coriander, cumin and chilli powder in a large bowl with 300 ml (½ pint) of the chicken stock. Add the peanut mixture to the chicken and cook for a further 5 minutes.

4 Add the tomatoes, chickpeas and a further 300 ml (½ pint) of the chicken stock and cook, covered, in a preheated oven, 190°C (375°F), Gas Mark 5, for about 25 minutes.

5 Remove the casserole lid and continue to cook for a further 20 minutes before serving sprinkled with chopped coriander leaves.

Nutrition note

Adding chickpeas to the dish means that you do not require as much meat and also lowers the GI.

POACHED GUINEA FOWL
with blueberry marmalade

Preparation time: 10 minutes

Cooking time: 1½ hours

Serves 4

1 guinea fowl, about 1 kg (2 lb)

600 ml (1 pint) Chicken Stock (see page 69)

1 bouquet garni

150 g (5 oz) blueberries

CARBOHYDRATE 3 g

FAT 15 g

PROTEIN 28 g

ENERGY 257 kcal/1072 kJ

1 Put the guinea fowl in a large saucepan with the chicken stock and bouquet garni. Add some water if necessary so that the liquid comes about two-thirds of the way up the bird. Bring to the boil and simmer gently for 1–1¼ hours until the meat is tender.

2 Lift the guinea fowl from the cooking liquid, carefully remove the skin, cover the bird with foil and keep hot.

3 Put 100 ml (3½ fl oz) of the stock in a small saucepan with the blueberries. Boil together rapidly for 10 minutes until the liquid is reduced but the blueberries are still intact.

4 Carve the guinea fowl by removing the breasts whole and cutting each in half. Remove the legs and cut each in half at the joint. In this way each person receives some breast and some darker meat.

5 Serve the meat with a large tablespoon of blueberry marmalade.

Nutrition notes

Blueberries are bursting with valuable antioxidants. Cooking them in the stock releases their sweetness, so no additional sugar is required.

Serve this dish with some low-GI vegetables, such as asparagus or steamed broccoli to lower the GI even further.

VENISON CASSEROLE

Preparation time: 15 minutes

Cooking time: 2 hours

Serves 4

2 onions, sliced

4 venison steaks, about 125 g (4 oz) each

1 bouquet garni

½ cinnamon stick

5 pickled walnuts, sliced

250 ml (8 fl oz) Beef Stock (see page 74)

3 tablespoons red wine

1 teaspoon Angostura bitters

4 large field or portobello mushrooms

2 tablespoons chopped parsley

CARBOHYDRATE 6 g

FAT 7 g

PROTEIN 30 g

ENERGY 225 kcal/946 kJ

1 Put the onions in a casserole dish and lay the venison steaks on top. Add the bouquet garni, cinnamon stick and sliced pickled walnuts. Pour over the beef stock, wine and Angostura bitters and cover. Cook in a preheated oven, 180°C (350°F), Gas Mark 4, for 1¾ hours until tender.

2 Remove the stalks from the mushrooms and wipe the caps clean. Add the mushroom caps, whole, to the casserole dish, covering them partially with the juices. Return the casserole to the oven for a further 15 minutes.

3 To serve, place a mushroom on each plate and top with a venison steak. Spoon the meat juices and onions on top and sprinkle with chopped parsley.

Nutrition notes

Venison is an extremely lean meat, which is great for low-fat diets. The delicious sauce in this recipe prevents it from drying out or becoming tough.

Boiled new potatoes and a steamed green vegetable, such as cabbage, are ideal accompaniments to this dish.

ROAST PHEASANT
with cabbage and apple rings

Preparation time: 20 minutes

Cooking time: 50 minutes

Serves 4

2 tablespoons vegetable oil

2 pheasants

100 g (3½ oz) pancetta, cut into matchsticks

2 garlic cloves, thinly sliced

150 ml (¼ pint) red wine

1 small Savoy cabbage, about 500 g (1 lb), quartered, hard inner stalk removed

300 ml (½ pint) Chicken Stock (see page 69)

APPLE RINGS

2 dessert apples, about 275 g (9 oz) in total, unpeeled, cored and cut into 1 cm (½ inch) thick rings

2 teaspoons vegetable oil

CARBOHYDRATE 13 g

FAT 29 g

PROTEIN 59 g

ENERGY 570 kcal/2385 kJ

1 Heat the oil in an nonstick roasting tin on the hob and brown the pheasants well on all sides over a medium-high heat for about 10 minutes.

2 Roast the pheasants, uncovered and breast side down, in a preheated oven, 230°C (450°F), Gas Mark 8, for 20 minutes. Remove the pheasants from the tin and set aside for 5 minutes.

3 Place the pancetta in the roasting tin and fry for 2–3 minutes on top of the hob until brown. Add the garlic and cook for 1 minute. Pour in the wine and boil to reduce. Separate the cabbage into leaves and add to the tin along with the stock.

4 Use a strong knife to cut the pheasants in half through the breastbone. Return the pheasant halves to the pancetta and cabbage mixture. Cover with foil and cook gently together over a low heat on top of the hob for 15 minutes.

5 Meanwhile, make the apple rings. Heat the oil in a nonstick frying pan and fry the apple rings for about 5 minutes until they are brown on each side.

6 Serve the pheasant halves on a bed of the cabbage mixture, with the juices as a gravy and decorated with the apple rings.

Nutrition notes

Savoy cabbage is rich in beta-carotene, an antioxidant that may help to prevent cell damage by free radicals.

The pancetta contains plenty of salt, so no additional salt is needed in this recipe.

BRAISED OXTAIL
with orange

Preparation time: 30 minutes

Cooking time: 3 hours

Serves 4

1 teaspoon vegetable oil

2 onions, sliced

1 oxtail, about 1 kg (2 lb), cut into pieces and trimmed of as much fat as possible

375 g (12 oz) carrots, sliced

600 g (1¼ lb) yellow swede, chopped into 4 large pieces

1 bouquet garni

1 tablespoon tomato purée

3 oranges, peeled, pith removed and sliced

BEEF STOCK

750 g (1½ lb) shin of lean beef, cubed

2 onions, chopped

2–3 carrots, chopped

1 bay leaf

1 bouquet garni

4–6 peppercorns

1.8 litres (3 pints) water

½ teaspoon salt

TO GARNISH

2 tablespoons chopped parsley

grated rind of 1 orange

CARBOHYDRATE 32 g

FAT 14 g

PROTEIN 32 g

ENERGY 376 kcal/1576 kJ

1 Make the beef stock. Put all the ingredients in a large saucepan. Bring to the boil slowly then immediately reduce the heat to a slow simmer. Cover the pan with a well-fitting lid and simmer for 4 hours, removing any scum that rises to the surface. Remove from the heat and strain the stock through a muslin-lined sieve and leave to cool before refrigerating. These ingredients will make about 1.5 litres (2½ pints). Any stock that is not used can be chilled then frozen for use in other recipes.

2 Meanwhile, heat the oil in a large, ovenproof pan on the hob. Add the onion to soften for 4–5 minutes.

3 Add the pieces of oxtail to the pan. Cook for 5 minutes until brown on all sides.

4 Add the carrot and swede to the pan and cook until they are lightly browned. Gradually stir in 500 ml (17 fl oz) of the stock and then add the bouquet garni, tomato purée and orange rounds. Heat the mixture to simmering.

5 Cover and cook in a preheated oven, 150°C (300°F), Gas Mark 2, for 2½–3 hours until the oxtail is tender. Remove the bouquet garni.

6 Serve the oxtail, garnished with chopped parsley and grated orange rind, together with the vegetables and sauce.

Nutrition notes

Keep the swede in as large pieces as possible and avoid mashing it, because this raises the GI.

Including both carrots and swede in the dish instead of potato means that it is easy to eat more of your recommended daily vegetable portions.

LOIN OF PORK
with artichoke hearts

Preparation time: 25 minutes
Cooking time: 1 hour 20 minutes
Serves 4

2 teaspoons olive oil
600 g (1¼ lb) boneless rolled loin of pork
50 ml (2 fl oz) dry white wine
150 ml (¼ pint) Vegetable Stock (see page 14)
2 large onions, sliced into thin rounds
4 tomatoes, skinned (see page 43) and quartered
425 g (14 oz) canned artichoke hearts, drained and quartered
2 teaspoons coriander seeds, lightly crushed
salt

TO SERVE
2 tablespoons chopped parsley
250 g (8 oz) basmati rice

CARBOHYDRATE 71 g
FAT 14 g
PROTEIN 41 g
ENERGY 565 kcal/2374 kJ

1 Heat the oil in an ovenproof casserole dish that can go on the hob and cook the pork gently for about 10 minutes, turning it so that it is evenly browned.

2 Add the wine and vegetable stock and bring to the boil before reducing the heat to a gentle simmer. Cover and cook in a preheated oven, 190°C (375°F), Gas Mark 5, for 40–50 minutes.

3 Remove the meat, cover it with foil and set aside. Return the casserole dish to the hob and bring the juices to the boil until they thicken slightly. (If few juices remain, add a little more vegetable stock to remove the flavours from the pan.)

4 Add the onions to the juices and cook until softened. Stir in the tomatoes, artichoke hearts and coriander seeds. Cover and cook on a medium-low heat for 8–10 minutes until the tomatoes soften.

5 Meanwhile, cook the basmati rice in lightly salted boiling water for 12–15 minutes or according to packet instructions.

6 Slice the pork and serve it, sprinkled with chopped parsley, with the artichoke hearts, tomato and onion mixture and basmati rice.

Nutrition note
Trimmed pork loin is a lean cut of meat and consequently lower in fat. Serve with basmati rice, one of the lowest GI varieties.

FILLET STEAK
with crunchy horseradish cream

Preparation time: 5 minutes
Cooking time: 2–12 minutes
Serves 4

1 teaspoon vegetable oil
fillet steak, about 500 g (1 lb) in total
shredded lettuce leaves, to serve

HORSERADISH CREAM
175 g (6 oz) reduced-fat Greek yogurt
65 g (2½ oz) shelled walnuts, chopped
40 g (1½ oz) horseradish sauce

CARBOHYDRATE 37 g
FAT 20 g
PROTEIN 30 g
ENERGY 322 kcal/1342 kJ

1 Make the horseradish cream. Mix together the yogurt, chopped walnuts and horseradish.

2 Heat a ridged griddle pan until it is hot and brush the surface with the oil.

3 Put the steaks on the grill and cook, turning once only to achieve a decorative ridged effect. The following timing is a rough guide for steaks that are about 2.5 cm (1 inch) thick. Blue: 1–2 minutes each side (soft with no feel of resistance); rare: 2–3 minutes each side (soft and spongy, may still ooze some red meat juices when pressed); medium rare: 3–4 minutes each side (a little firmer); medium: 4–5 minutes each side (firm to touch); well done: over 5 minutes each side (solid).

4 Serve the steaks accompanied by the horseradish cream and shredded lettuce leaves.

Nutrition note
Walnuts are a great source of protein and healthy omega-3 fats.

CITRUS ROAST DUCK
on wilted spinach leaves

Preparation time: 20 minutes

Cooking time: 1½ hours

Serves 4

1 duck, about 2 kg (4 lb) with giblets, giblets removed and duck washed and dried with kitchen paper

10 g (½ oz) unsalted butter

2 shallots, finely sliced

250 g (8 oz) baby spinach leaves

1 tablespoon thyme leaves

sea salt

black pepper

mandarin segments, to garnish

CITRUS SAUCE

3 mandarins

50 ml (2 fl oz) port

300 ml (½ pint) Chicken Stock (see page 69)

lemon juice, to taste

CARBOHYDRATE 8 g

FAT 14 g

PROTEIN 29 g

ENERGY 282 kcal/1180 kJ

1 Either put a roasting rack in an oven tray or line an oven tray with crumpled foil so that the fat can drain from the duck during roasting.

2 Prick the duck all over with a skewer and put it on the rack or foil in the oven tray. Season well with sea salt and black pepper and roast the duck in a preheated oven, 230°C (450°F), Gas Mark 8, for 1–1½ hours, draining the fat frequently during cooking. Do not baste. Check that the juices run clear at the end of the cooking time by inserting a skewer into the fattest part of a leg.

3 Meanwhile, make the citrus sauce. Grate the rind from the mandarins. Peel the mandarins, remove the pith and pips and liquidize the flesh until smooth. Mix together the mandarin pulp, rind, port and stock in a saucepan and boil until the sauce thickens slightly. Stir in lemon juice to taste.

4 Melt the butter in a large frying pan and pan-fry the shallots until softened. Add the spinach and thyme and cook until the leaves have wilted.

5 Serve the spinach leaves on a warm plate, lay the cooked duck on top and coat with the citrus sauce. Garnish with mandarin segments.

Nutrition note

Duck is very high in fat, but cooking in this way allows some of the fat to drain away. Do not use the juices for gravy because they are rich in less healthy saturated fat.

PAN-FRIED CALVES' LIVER
with pears

Preparation time: 15 minutes, plus
marinating and soaking

Cooking time: 4–5 minutes

Serves 4

2 large Comice pears, unpeeled, quartered,
cored and thinly sliced

1 teaspoon balsamic vinegar

375 g (12 oz) calves' liver, sliced thinly

3 tablespoons semi-skimmed milk

50 g (2 oz) wild rocket leaves

100 g (3½ oz) baby spinach leaves

40 g (1½ oz) pecan nuts, chopped

1 teaspoon vegetable oil

DRESSING

2 teaspoons balsamic vinegar

1 teaspoon chilli-infused olive oil

CARBOHYDRATE 16 g

FAT 16 g

PROTEIN 22 g

ENERGY 290 kcal/1214 kJ

1 Place the pear slices in a dish, sprinkle over the balsamic vinegar and leave to marinate.

2 Put the calves' liver in a flat dish and pour over the milk, then soak for 30 minutes to remove any bitterness.

3 Meanwhile, mix the dressing ingredients together. Toss the rocket and baby spinach leaves in the dressing. Arrange the leaves on individual plates and arrange slices of marinated pear on top. Sprinkle over the chopped pecans.

4 Discard the milk and pat the liver dry on kitchen paper. Heat the oil in a nonstick frying pan and pan-fry the liver for about 2 minutes on each side (depending on the thickness of the liver) until it is brown.

5 Serve the hot liver on top of the dressed salad.

Nutrition note

Serving a good helping of salad leaves and nuts alongside the liver lowers the GI of the meal as well as providing important antioxidant vitamins and minerals.

Vegetarian Creations

GARLIC, ROASTED PEPPER AND WALNUT PAPPARDELLE

Preparation time: 10–15 minutes

Cooking time: 35 minutes

Serves 4

2 teaspoons olive oil

4 red peppers, cored, deseeded and sliced

3–4 large garlic cloves, thinly sliced

60 g (2½ oz) walnuts, chopped

300 g (10 oz) fresh egg pappardelle

25 g (1 oz) Parmesan cheese shavings

salt and black pepper

CARBOHYDRATE 63 g

FAT 16 g

PROTEIN 15 g

ENERGY 435 kcal/1833 kJ

1 Use ½ teaspoon of the olive oil to brush over the peppers. Put the peppers on a baking sheet and roast them in a preheated oven, 230°C (450°F), Gas Mark 8, for 20–25 minutes until they are soft and just beginning to blacken.

2 Reserve 4 slices of pepper to use as a garnish and cut the remaining peppers into large dice.

3 Heat the remaining olive oil in a large frying pan over a medium-low heat, add the sliced garlic but do not let it brown. Add the diced red pepper and stir in the walnuts. Keep warm.

4 Bring a large saucepan of lightly salted water to the boil. Add the pasta, return to the boil and cook for 3–4 minutes or until the pasta is *al dente*. Drain and transfer to a large, warm serving bowl.

5 Toss the pasta well with the garlic, pepper and walnut mixture. Sprinkle over the Parmesan shavings and garnish with the reserved pepper slices.

Nutrition note

Walnuts contain healthy mono-unsaturated fats and a range of vitamins and minerals. Teaming them with fresh egg pasta, which can be lower in GI than normal pasta, makes a winning combination.

RUSTIC PASTA

Preparation time: 20 minutes

Cooking time: 20 minutes

Serves 4

500 g (1 lb) broccoli, cut into florets

2 teaspoons olive oil

1 large onion, finely chopped

1 garlic clove, crushed

400 g (13 oz) tomatoes, skinned (see page 43) and chopped

1 tablespoon tomato purée

125 g (4 oz) pitted black olives in herb-flavoured brine, drained

2 tablespoons chopped thyme

300 g (10 oz) dried wholewheat pasta shapes, such as fusilli

6 Darjeeling teabags

125 g (4 oz) reduced-fat buffalo mozzarella cheese, torn into small pieces

black pepper

TO SERVE

4 tomatoes, sliced

handful of basil leaves, torn

2 tablespoons balsamic vinegar

CARBOHYDRATE 64 g

FAT 12 g

PROTEIN 25 g

ENERGY 446 kcal/1883 kJ

1 Cook the broccoli florets in boiling water for about 3 minutes until just tender. Drain.

2 Meanwhile, heat the oil in a large frying pan and gently cook the onion and garlic until they are soft.

3 Add the tomatoes, tomato purée, olives, broccoli and thyme and cook for about 3 minutes. Season with black pepper and keep warm.

4 Bring a large saucepan of lightly salted water to the boil. Add the pasta and teabags, return to the boil and cook for 8–10 minutes or until the pasta is *al dente*. Discard the teabags and drain the pasta.

5 Toss the pasta in the broccoli sauce and add the chunks of torn mozzarella. Serve immediately in warm bowls with the sliced tomatoes and basil leaves and drizzled with balsamic vinegar.

Nutrition notes

Wholewheat pasta retains its beneficial fibre when cooked.

The broccoli and olives enhance the nutritional value of this dish.

PENNE
with olives and sun-dried tomatoes

Preparation time: 10 minutes

Cooking time: 8–12 minutes

Serves 4

250 g (8 oz) dried penne

125 g (4 oz) peas

1 tablespoon olive oil

2 garlic cloves, crushed

4 shallots, finely chopped

1 green pepper, cored, deseeded and diced

10 g (½ oz) mint, chopped

25 g (1 oz) basil leaves, chopped

125 g (4 oz) sun-dried tomatoes in oil, drained and sliced

50 g (2 oz) pitted black olives

1 tablespoon capers, chopped

150 ml (¼ pint) reduced-fat crème fraîche

salt and black pepper

CARBOHYDRATE 56 g

FAT 28 g

PROTEIN 14 g

ENERGY 515 kcal/2156 kJ

1 Bring a large pan of lightly salted water to the boil. Add the pasta, return to the boil and cook for 8–10 minutes or until the pasta is *al dente*.

2 Meanwhile, cook the peas in lightly salted boiling water for 5 minutes.

3 Heat the oil in a large nonstick frying pan. Add the garlic, shallots, pepper and peas and fry for about 5 minutes until the onions are light brown and the peppers are just cooked.

4 Drain the pasta. Add the herbs, tomatoes, olives, capers and cooked pasta to the frying pan. Season to taste. Heat through, stir in the crème fraîche and serve immediately.

Nutrition note
Pasta is an excellent low-GI food to use as the basis of meals because it is absorbed slowly by the body, which makes it very sustaining.

GARLIC LINGUINI
and wild porcini

Preparation time: 15–20 minutes, plus soaking

Cooking time: 5–10 minutes

Serves 2

25 g (1 oz) dried porcini mushrooms

250 g (8 oz) fresh linguini

2 tablespoons olive oil

4 shallots, sliced

4 garlic cloves, thinly sliced

2 carrots, grated

1 heaped teaspoon dried oregano

50 g (2 oz) coriander leaves and stems, chopped

1 garlic clove, crushed

40 g (1½ oz) Parmesan cheese, finely grated

2 teaspoons extra virgin olive oil, to serve

oregano leaves, to garnish

CARBOHYDRATE 114 g

FAT 24 g

PROTEIN 26 g

ENERGY 743 kcal/3127 kJ

1 Soak the mushrooms in a bowl of warm water for 30 minutes. Drain and reserve the mushroom liquor.

2 Make the mushroom liquor up to about 1.5 litres (2½ pints) with water, transfer to a large pan and bring to the boil. Add the pasta, return to the boil and cook for 2 minutes or until the pasta is *al dente*.

3 Heat the oil in a large, nonstick pan and fry the shallots and sliced garlic for a few minutes.

4 Add the soaked mushrooms, carrots, dried oregano and coriander and stir-fry for 1–2 minutes. Add a few tablespoons of hot water if the mixture begins to stick to the bottom of the pan.

5 Drain the pasta and stir it into the vegetable mixture with the crushed garlic and half the Parmesan. Heat through and serve drizzled with extra virgin olive oil and sprinkled with the remaining Parmesan cheese and the oregano leaves.

Nutrition notes

Grating a strong cheese such as Parmesan will encourage you to use less and therefore keep down your intake of saturated fat.

Garlic has been shown to help thin the blood and hence protect against heart disease.

INDIVIDUAL DHAL SOUFFLÉS

Preparation time: 15 minutes

Cooking time: 1¼ hours

Serves 4

20 g (¾ oz) butter

30 g (1¼ oz) plain flour

600 ml (1 pint) skimmed milk

yolks of 2 large eggs

whites of 4 large eggs

2 tablespoons chopped chives

1 teaspoon vegetable oil

green salad, to serve

SPICED DHAL

1 teaspoon cumin seeds

225 g (7½ oz) moong dhal, washed until water runs clear

1 small onion, sliced

2 cinnamon sticks

1 small chilli, deseeded and chopped

salt and black pepper

CARBOHYDRATE 48 g

FAT 9 g

PROTEIN 24 g

ENERGY 365 kcal/1527 kJ

1 Make the spiced dhal. Toast the cumin seeds in a dry pan over medium heat until they start to pop. Put the moong dhal in saucepan and add sufficient water to cover, bring to the boil and simmer rapidly for 15 minutes. Drain the dhal, rinsing in hot water.

2 Return the dhal to the saucepan with the onion and cinnamon sticks. Add sufficient hot water to cover the dhal by about 1 cm (½ inch). Bring back to the boil, reduce the heat and simmer gently for 25–30 minutes. Drain off any excess liquid and discard the cinnamon sticks. Add the chilli, a pinch of salt, a liberal amount of black pepper and the toasted cumin seeds. Mix well.

3 Melt the butter in a saucepan and stir in the flour. Cook, stirring, for 1–2 minutes. Meanwhile, warm the milk in a separate saucepan. Remove from the heat and whisk in the warm milk until the sauce is smooth. Return to the heat and continue whisking until the sauce thickens.

4 Mix the white sauce into the spiced dhal and stir in the egg yolks.

5 Beat the egg whites in a large bowl until firm and gently stir one-third into the spiced mixture. Fold in the remainder of the egg whites with a metal spoon. Mix in the chives.

6 Lightly grease 4 ramekin dishes with the oil. Pour the egg and dhal mixture into the ramekins and cook in a preheated oven, 190°F (375°F), Gas Mark 5, for 15–20 minutes until they begin to brown and are firm to the touch. Serve immediately with a green salad.

Nutrition note

Pulses are a great source of soluble fibre and keep the GI of a meal low. This is especially true of this recipe as the lentils (moong dhal) are not pureéd.

ALMOND AND APRICOT WILD RICE
with cumin seeds

Preparation time: 20 minutes, plus soaking

Cooking time: 20 minutes

Serves 4

300 g (10 oz) long grain and wild rice

2 tablespoons olive oil

3 shallots, quartered

2 garlic cloves, crushed

2 teaspoons cumin seeds

4 red and 4 black peppercorns

50 g (2 oz) whole almonds, toasted

300 g (10 oz) can borlotti beans, drained

100 g (3½ oz) ready-to-eat apricots, roughly chopped

½ teaspoon ground turmeric

800 ml (1¼ pints) Vegetable Stock, lightly salted (see page 14)

4 spring onions, green stems only, sliced

15 g (½ oz) mint, roughly chopped

salt and black pepper

TO SERVE

2 tablespoons lemon juice

25 g (1 oz) Parmesan cheese, grated

1–2 teaspoons red chilli powder (optional)

200 g (7 oz) reduced-fat Greek yogurt

CARBOHYDRATE 120 g

FAT 17 g

PROTEIN 16 g

ENERGY 538 kcal/2270 kJ

1 Wash and soak the rice in a bowl of cold water while you prepare the other ingredients.

2 Heat the oil in a large, heavy-based pan with a lid. Fry the shallots and garlic for 1–2 minutes, then add the cumin seeds and peppercorns and stir-fry for a few seconds.

3 Chop half the almonds, reserving the rest for garnish. Add the chopped almonds, beans, apricots, turmeric and stock to the pan and stir thoroughly.

4 Stir in the drained rice, cover and simmer for 15 minutes. Add the spring onions and mint, check the seasoning and stir gently. Add a little hot water if the pan is dry and the rice is not fully cooked. Allow to cook, covered, for a further 3 minutes.

5 Serve with a drizzle of lemon juice, a sprinkling of Parmesan cheese, the remaining almonds and chilli powder, if using. Offer the yogurt separately.

Nutrition notes

Different types of rice have different GI values. Risotto rice tends to have the highest GI, so try not to use it too often.

The beans, apricots, lemon and almonds in this recipe will help to keep the GI low.

PEA AND MINT FRITTATA

Preparation time: 20 minutes

Cooking time: 10 minutes

Serves 4

200 g (7 oz) sweet potato, sliced

100 g (3½ oz) peas

1 tablespoon olive oil

2 shallots, finely sliced

1 red pepper, cored, deseeded and thinly sliced lengthways

6 eggs, beaten

1 tablespoon skimmed milk

1 tablespoon freshly grated Parmesan cheese

4 tablespoons chopped mint

frisée lettuce leaves, to serve

black pepper

CARBOHYDRATE 16 g

FAT 13 g

PROTEIN 14 g

ENERGY 235 kcal/980 kJ

1 Cook the sweet potato and peas in a saucepan of boiling water for 4–5 minutes until tender. Drain.

2 Heat the oil in a deep, nonstick frying pan and stir-fry the shallots and red pepper over a moderate heat for 1–2 minutes. Stir in the peas and sweet potatoes and warm through for a further 2 minutes.

3 Combine the eggs with the milk and Parmesan and season to taste with black pepper. Pour the egg mixture over the vegetables, lifting the vegetables slightly so that the egg runs to the bottom of the pan. Cook gently over a low heat and lightly stir in the mint.

4 Preheat the grill to medium-hot and cook the top of the frittata for 3–4 minutes until it is brown and fluffy. Remove, cut into wedges and serve with a grind of black pepper and accompanied by frisée lettuce leaves.

Nutrition notes

The Parmesan in this recipe provides a salty flavour, so you don't need to add extra salt.

Using vegetables that are different colours helps to provide a varied range of nutrients: betacarotene from the sweet potato and B vitamins and vitamin C from the peas. Weight for weight, the red peppers contain three times as much vitamin C as an orange.

SPEEDY KIDNEY BEAN AND CORIANDER CURRY

Preparation time: 5 minutes

Cooking time: 5 minutes

Serves 4

2 teaspoons corn oil

1 teaspoon cumin seeds

1 tablespoon tomato purée

2 teaspoons curry powder

1 teaspoon ground turmeric

1 teaspoon ground coriander

1 teaspoon ground cumin

2 teaspoons garam masala

410 g (13¼ oz) can kidney beans, drained

2 spring onions, sliced

2 tablespoons chopped coriander leaves

salt

mixed salad leaves or pitta breads, to serve

CARBOHYDRATE 21 g

FAT 3 g

PROTEIN 8 g

ENERGY 136 kcal/572 kJ

1 Heat the oil in a nonstick pan. Add the cumin seeds and let them pop for a few seconds.

2 Stir in the tomato purée, curry powder, ground spices and garam masala and blend well together over a low heat.

3 Mix in the kidney beans, spring onions and coriander leaves. Add salt to taste and stir in a few tablespoons of hot water if you prefer more sauce. Serve hot with a mixed salad leaves or in pitta breads.

Nutrition note

Beans and lentils are high in soluble fibre, which helps you control blood glucose levels more easily. This type of fibre has also been shown to lower blood fats, such as cholesterol. Try to eat two large helpings of beans or lentils every day.

SPICY SCRAMBLED EGG
with onion and red pepper

Preparation time: 5 minutes
Cooking time: 5–10 minutes
Serves 4

1 tablespoon olive oil
1 tablespoon sesame oil
1 large onion, sliced
1 red pepper, cored, deseeded and sliced
1 teaspoon cumin seeds
1 teaspoon crushed ginger
8 eggs
2 tablespoons water
salt and black pepper

TO SERVE
2 wholemeal pitta breads
2 tablespoons sweet chilli dipping sauce
10 chive stalks, snipped

CARBOHYDRATE 21 g
FAT 18 g
PROTEIN 19 g
ENERGY 320 kcal/1344 kJ

1 Heat the oils in a frying pan and fry the onion and pepper for 2–3 minutes over a moderate heat until they are soft but not browned. Stir in the cumin seeds and ginger and fry for 1 minute

2 Beat the eggs and the measurement water and season to taste. Add the eggs to the pan and stir-fry for about 2 minutes until lightly scrambled and just cooked.

3 Meanwhile, toast the pitta breads, then cut into diagonal strips and serve with the spicy scrambled egg. Drizzle the dipping sauce around the outside and garnish with snipped chives.

Nutrition note
Although eggs contain cholesterol, dietary cholesterol does not have a significant effect on blood cholesterol. So, unless you have been advised otherwise, it is fine to have about five eggs each week as part of an overall balanced diet.

MEDITERRANEAN PEPPERS

Preparation time: 10 minutes

Cooking time: 1 hour

Serves 4

2 red and 2 yellow peppers, halved, cored and deseeded but stems left intact

24 cherry tomatoes, halved

2 garlic cloves, thinly sliced

1 bunch basil

40 g (1½ oz) capers in brine, drained and rinsed

25 ml (1 fl oz) olive oil

black pepper

mixed salad leaves, to serve

CARBOHYDRATE 10 g

FAT 8 g

PROTEIN 5 g

ENERGY 128 kcal/535 kJ

1 Place the mixed peppers, cut side up, in a shallow baking dish.

2 Divide the halved cherry tomatoes, slivers of garlic and capers between the pepper halves. Add a few basil leaves then lightly drizzle each pepper with olive oil and season with black pepper.

3 Pour 300 ml (½ pint) water into the base of the dish to prevent the peppers from sticking. Cover tightly with foil and cook in a preheated oven, 180°C (350°F), Gas Mark 4, for 20 minutes. Remove the foil, reduce the temperature to 150°C (300°F), Gas Mark 2, and bake for another 40 minutes until soft.

4 Garnish the peppers with the remaining basil leaves and serve with mixed salad leaves.

Nutrition notes

Red and yellow peppers are rich in betacarotene, which is converted to the antioxidant vitamin A in the body.

Olive oil, an integral part of the Mediterranean diet, is high in unsaturated fats, which are beneficial for your heart.

RED LENTIL DHAL
with cucumber raita

Preparation time: 15 minutes

Cooking time: 30 minutes

Serves 4

225 g (7½ oz) red lentils

1 tablespoon rapeseed oil

1 large onion, finely chopped

2 garlic cloves, crushed

1 teaspoon crushed ginger

2 green chillies, deseeded and finely chopped

4 tomatoes, finely chopped

½ teaspoon ground turmeric

1½ teaspoons garam masala

450 ml (¾ pint) hot water

4 tablespoons lemon juice

50 g (2 oz) coriander leaves and stems, chopped

salt

pitta breads, to serve

RAITA

10 cm (4 inches) cucumber, grated

450 ml (¾ pint) reduced-fat natural yogurt

1 teaspoon cumin seeds

½ teaspoon black pepper

TO GARNISH

3 spring onions, green stems only, sliced diagonally

½ teaspoon red chilli powder

CARBOHYDRATE 48 g

FAT 5 g

PROTEIN 22 g

ENERGY 316 kcal/1336 kJ

1 Soak the lentils in a bowl of warm water. Heat the oil in a large, nonstick frying pan with a lid. Stir-fry the onion, garlic, ginger and chillies for 3–5 minutes. Stir in the tomatoes and cook, stirring occasionally, until the tomatoes begin to go mushy. Add the turmeric and garam masala. Cover and simmer, stirring occasionally, for 5 minutes.

2 Drain the lentils and add them, with the measurement water to the frying pan. Stir well, cover and cook for 15–20 minutes until the dhal is tender but not mushy. Add a little more water if the dhal is too dry.

3 Meanwhile, make the raita. Drain the grated cucumber on kitchen paper and add this to the other ingredients. Chill until ready to serve.

4 When the dhal is cooked, gently stir in salt to taste, lemon juice and coriander. Garnish with the spring onions and sprinkle red chilli powder over the raita. Serve with pitta breads.

Nutrition notes

This dish is a good source of soluble fibre and lycopene.

Vegetarian meals can often be low in iron; the garam masala in this recipe will provide some iron, and combining it with the vitamin C from the fresh coriander and lime juice will enhance the rate at which it is absorbed.

QUORN™ AND CASHEW STIR-FRY

Preparation time: 10 minutes

Cooking time: 20 minutes

Serves 4

2 tablespoons rapeseed oil

1 onion, sliced lengthways

2 teaspoons crushed ginger

100 g (3½ oz) cashew nuts

300 g (10 oz) mangetout

250 g (8 oz) Quorn™ pieces

2 tablespoons soy sauce

150 g (5 oz) mixed oyster and shiitake mushrooms

2 teaspoons five spice powder

250 g (8 oz) baby sweetcorn

200 g (7 oz) pak choi, shredded

4 spring onions, sliced diagonally

1 teaspoon black pepper

2 tablespoons chopped flat leaf parsley

2 tablespoons chopped mint

2 teaspoons sesame seeds, to serve

CARBOHYDRATE 16 g

FAT 21 g

PROTEIN 21 g

ENERGY 334 kcal/1389 kJ

1 Heat the oil in a nonstick wok or large frying pan and stir-fry the onion, ginger, cashew nuts and mangetout for a few minutes.

2 Stir in the Quorn™, soy sauce, mushrooms and five spice powder. Stir-fry for 7–10 minutes until almost cooked and then add the baby sweetcorn. Stir-fry for 2 minutes more before adding the pak choi. Add a few tablespoons of hot water from time to time to prevent burning.

3 Add the remaining ingredients, cook through, check the seasoning and serve sprinkled with the sesame seeds.

Nutrition note

Quorn™ is a tasty and low-fat way to enjoy vegetarian meals. It absorbs flavours well and cooks in minutes.

STIR-FRIED NOODLES
with field mushrooms

Preparation time: 10 minutes

Cooking time: 10 minutes

Serves 4

225 g (7½ oz) thread egg noodles

1 tablespoon corn oil

1 large onion, sliced lengthways

1 cm (½ inch) fresh root ginger, finely chopped

200 g (7 oz) field or portobello mushrooms

125 g (4 oz) bean sprouts

2 large red peppers, cored, deseeded and thinly sliced

1 tablespoon plum sauce

2 tablespoons light soy sauce

6 spring onions, sliced diagonally into 2 cm (¾ inch) pieces

CARBOHYDRATE 53 g

FAT 8 g

PROTEIN 11 g

ENERGY 317 kcal/1336 kJ

1 Cook the noodles in a pan of boiling water for 3–4 minutes. Drain, rinse and set aside.

2 Meanwhile, heat the oil in a wok or large frying pan and stir-fry the onion and ginger for 2–3 minutes. Add the mushrooms and cook for 1–2 minutes over a medium heat.

3 Stir in the bean sprouts, peppers, plum sauce, soy sauce and spring onions and cook for a further few minutes, stiring occasionally.

4 Mix in the noodles, adjust the seasoning and heat through before serving.

Nutrition notes

Stir-frying is a quick method of cooking that helps to preserve nutrients.

Don't be tempted to add salt – the soy sauce in this recipe makes it salty enough.

BULGUR WHEAT SALAD
with spiced yogurt

Preparation time: 20 minutes, plus soaking and resting

Serves 2

125 g (4 oz) bulgur wheat

4 large plums, pitted and each cut into about 8 slices

1 garlic clove, crushed

1 red onion, finely chopped

25 g (1 oz) flat leaf parsley, chopped

handful of mint, chopped

2 tablespoons olive oil

4 tablespoons lemon juice

salt and black pepper

SPICED YOGURT

4 tablespoons reduced-fat natural yogurt

1 garlic clove, crushed

½ teaspoon cayenne pepper

½ teaspoon tomato purée

finely chopped chives, to garnish

CARBOHYDRATE 38 g

FAT 7 g

PROTEIN 6 g

ENERGY 230 kcal/965 kJ

1 Place the bulgur wheat in a large bowl, cover it with water and leave for 30 minutes to swell up.

2 Drain away any excess water from the bulgur wheat and squeeze it dry with your hands.

3 Mix in all the other ingredients and put the salad in the refrigerator to rest for at least 30 minutes to allow the flavours to develop.

4 Make the spiced yogurt. Mix together all the ingredients and garnish with finely chopped chives.

5 Serve the bulgur wheat salad accompanied by the spiced yogurt.

Nutrition notes

Bulgur wheat is a great alternative to rice and has a lower GI.

Plums make a refreshing addition to this dish and also help to keep down the GI.

CHICKPEA AND OLIVE SALAD

Preparation time: 10 minutes

Serves **4**

250 g (8 oz) can chickpeas, drained

50 g (2 oz) pitted black olives, halved

½ red onion, finely chopped

150 g (5 oz) cherry tomatoes, halved

3 tablespoons chopped flat leaf parsley, plus extra to garnish

50 g (2 oz) watercress leaves, to serve

DRESSING

1 garlic clove, crushed

100 ml (3½ fl oz) reduced-fat Greek yogurt

juice of ½ lime

black pepper

CARBOHYDRATE 33 g

FAT 4 g

PROTEIN 7 g

ENERGY 122 kcal/516 kJ

1 Make the dressing. Mix together the garlic, yogurt and lime juice. Season to taste with black pepper.

2 Stir together the chickpeas, olives, onion, tomatoes and parsley.

3 Add the dressing to the chickpea mixture, mix thoroughly, and serve on a bed of watercress leaves, garnished with chopped parsley.

Nutrition note

Chickpeas are high in soluble fibre. This type of fibre is thought to help lower raised blood cholesterol levels.

Sumptuous
Sides

GINGER BROCCOLI
with fennel seeds

Preparation time: 5 minutes
Cooking time: 5 minutes
Serves 4

2 teaspoons olive oil
1 teaspoon crushed ginger
½ teaspoon fennel seeds
500 g (1 lb) broccoli florets
3 tablespoons reduced-salt soy sauce
black pepper, to taste

CARBOHYDRATE 4 g
FAT 3 g
PROTEIN 7 g
ENERGY 64 kcal/267 kJ

1 Heat the oil in a nonstick wok or frying pan and stir-fry the ginger and fennel seeds over a medium heat for a few seconds.

2 Add the broccoli, soy sauce and black pepper and stir-fry until the broccoli is just cooked.

Nutrition note
One serving of this dish provides just over one portion of the recommended five-a-day servings of vegetables.

RED CABBAGE COLESLAW

Preparation time: 10 minutes, plus chilling

Serves 4

225 g (7½ oz) red cabbage, shredded or grated

4 carrots, grated

3 spring onions, sliced

3 tablespoons chopped flat leaf parsley

2 tablespoons shredded basil leaves

100 ml (3½ fl oz) reduced-calorie mayonnaise

50 ml (2 fl oz) reduced-fat natural yogurt

CARBOHYDRATE 12 g

FAT 8 g

PROTEIN 2 g

ENERGY 125 kcal/520 kJ

1   Mix all the ingredients together. Chill for 20–30 minutes before serving.

Nutrition note

The reduced-calorie mayonnaise used here helps to keep the fat content lower than in standard coleslaw, and the reduced-fat natural yogurt adds creaminess without piling on the fat.

COURGETTE RONDELLES

Preparation time: 5 minutes

Cooking time: 10 minutes

Serves 4

1 tablespoon olive oil

pinch of reduced-salt vegetable bouillon powder

2 yellow and 2 green courgettes, thinly sliced into rounds

½ teaspoon crushed dried chillies

2 tablespoons lemon juice

TO GARNISH

16 baby plum tomatoes, cut in half lengthways

coriander leaves, chopped

CARBOHYDRATE 5 g

FAT 3 g

PROTEIN 2 g

ENERGY 50 kcal/215 kJ

1 Heat the oil in a large, nonstick frying pan. Add the vegetable bouillon powder and stir until well blended.

2 Add the thinly sliced courgettes and sauté over a medium heat for 5–8 minutes until they take on an intense green-yellow colour. Do not brown.

3 Season with the crushed dried chillies and lemon juice and serve garnished with the baby plum tomatoes and coriander leaves.

FRAGRANT CINNAMON BASMATI RICE

Preparation time: 2 hours, 5 minutes, plus soaking

Cooking time: 18–20 minutes

Serves 4

250 g (8 oz) basmati rice

1 litre (1¾ pints) water, for soaking

500 ml (17 fl oz) water, for cooking

200 g (7 oz) peas

2 teaspoons cumin seeds

4 sticks cinnamon, each broken into 2–3 pieces

3 black cardamom pods

3 star anise

1 teaspoon salt

5 g (¼ oz) butter

CARBOHYDRATE 60 g

FAT 3 g

PROTEIN 8 g

ENERGY 280 kcal/1195 kJ

1 Wash the rice in several changes of water. Then soak the rice in a large bowl filled with the measurement soaking water for 2 hours.

2 Drain the rice then put it with all the other ingredients into a large pan and pour in the measurement cooking water. Cover with a tight-fitting lid.

3 Cook over a medium heat for 18–20 minutes, stirring gently halfway through cooking.

Nutrition note
Basmati rice has one of the lowest GI ratings of all types of rice.

CARAMELIZED FRENCH BEANS

Preparation time: 5 minutes

Cooking time: 12–15 minutes

Serves 2

2 teaspoons olive oil

1 garlic clove, crushed

200 g (7 oz) fine green beans, topped and tailed

1 tablespoon thyme leaves

3 tablespoons balsamic vinegar

2 tablespoons soy sauce, or salt to taste

¼ teaspoon black pepper

1 teaspoon sesame seeds, to serve

CARBOHYDRATE 5 g

FAT 4 g

PROTEIN 4 g

ENERGY 74 kcal/307 kJ

1 Heat the oil in a nonstick frying pan, add the garlic and the beans and stir-fry over a medium heat for 2–3 minutes.

2 Stir in the thyme leaves, balsamic vinegar and soy sauce (or salt) and black pepper. Cook for 10–12 minutes, until the beans are just cooked, adding a few tablespoons of hot water if the beans begin to stick to the bottom.

3 Serve sprinkled with the sesame seeds.

Nutrition note

Cooking fresh vegetables quickly, so that they still have some 'bite', helps to preserve the nutrients.

SWEET POTATO AND CHILLI MASH

Preparation time: 10 minutes

Cooking time: 15 minutes

Serves 4

3 sweet potatoes, about 875 g (1¾ lb) in total, chopped

5 g (¼ oz) butter

2 tablespoons semi-skimmed milk

15 g (½ oz) chives, snipped

1–2 tablespoons sweet chilli sauce

CARBOHYDRATE 47 g

FAT 2 g

PROTEIN 3 g

ENERGY 205 kcal/874 kJ

1 Place the sweet potatoes in a saucepan of water, bring to the boil and cook for about 15 minutes until soft. Drain the potatoes and return them to the saucepan.

2 Mash the potatoes with all the other ingredients and serve immediately.

FRUITY COUSCOUS
with lime

Preparation time: 5 minutes

Cooking time: 12 minutes

Serves 4

400 ml (14 fl oz) Vegetable Stock (see page 14)

200 g (7 oz) couscous

1 tablespoon olive oil

1 red onion, chopped

1 red pepper, cored, deseeded and chopped

10 g (½ oz) flat leaf parsley, chopped

10 g (½ oz) basil leaves, torn

10 g (½ oz) mint, chopped

juice and rind of 1 lime

50 g (2 oz) ready-to-eat apricots, chopped

pinch of ground cinnamon

25 g (1 oz) toasted flaked almonds

CARBOHYDRATE 36 g

FAT 7 g

PROTEIN 6 g

ENERGY 223 kcal/930 kJ

1 Heat the vegetable stock in a pan with a lid. Add the couscous, cover and leave to swell for about 6 minutes.

2 Meanwhile, heat the oil in a frying pan and gently soften the onion and pepper over a moderate heat for 3 minutes.

3 Stir the cooked onion into the couscous with all the other ingredients. Heat through for 5 minutes and serve hot or cold.

Nutrition note

Couscous makes a refreshing change to rice and it offers a medium GI rating.

CUCUMBER AND TOMATO SALSA

Preparation time: 10 minutes

Serves 4

15 cm (6 inch) cucumber, finely diced

1 orange pepper, cored, deseeded and finely chopped

2 spring onions, green stems only, finely sliced

6 vine-ripened tomatoes, finely diced

juice of 1 lime

2 tablespoons chopped flat leaf parsley

2 tablespoons chopped mint

salt and black pepper

CARBOHYDRATE 7 g

FAT 1 g

PROTEIN 2 g

ENERGY 36 kcal/155 kJ

1 Mix together the cucumber, orange pepper, spring onions and tomatoes.

2 Make a dressing by combining the lime juice, herbs and seasoning.

3 Stir the dressing into the vegetables and pile into a serving bowl.

Nutrition note

The raw fruit and vegetables in this salsa are packed with vitamins. This dish boasts vitamin C and betacarotene, both of which are valuable antioxidants.

SAUTÉED OKRA
with onion seeds and saffron

Preparation time: 10 minutes

Cooking time: 25 minutes

Serves 4

3 tablespoons olive oil

1 teaspoon onion seeds

1 garlic clove, crushed

1 teaspoon crushed ginger

500 g (1 lb) okra, topped and tailed

a good pinch of saffron

1 teaspoon curry powder

½ teaspoon salt

TO SERVE

2 teaspoons sesame seeds

2 tablespoons chopped coriander leaves

CARBOHYDRATE 5 g

FAT 11 g

PROTEIN 4 g

ENERGY 129 kcal/536 kJ

1 Heat the oil in a nonstick pan and add the onion seeds. Fry over a moderate heat for a few seconds before stirring in the garlic and ginger.

2 Add the okra and flavourings and cook, uncovered, for about 20 minutes until tender. Stir occasionally. Add small amounts of hot water if the okra begin to stick to the bottom of the pan.

3 Serve immediately sprinkled with sesame seeds and coriander leaves.

Nutrition note

Cooking for less time helps to keep the GI low because the okra are nearer their firm, raw state.

FIVE-MINUTE BABY SWEETCORN
with coriander

Preparation time: 5 minutes

Cooking time: 5 minutes

Serves 4

1 teaspoon whole coriander seeds

1 tablespoon olive oil

250 g (8 oz) baby sweetcorn

good pinch of black pepper

2 teaspoons ground turmeric

30 g (1¼ oz) coriander leaves, finely chopped

2 tablespoons lemon juice

CARBOHYDRATE 2 g

FAT 3 g

PROTEIN 2 g

ENERGY 48 kcal/198 kJ

1 Lightly crush the coriander seeds with a rolling pin or using a pestle and mortar. Heat the oil in a wok or frying pan, add the coriander seeds and stir-fry for a few seconds.

2 Stir in the sweetcorn with the black pepper and turmeric and cook for 3–4 minutes. Add the coriander leaves.

3 Add the lemon juice and allow to sizzle in the pan just before serving.

Nutrition note
Baby sweetcorn, weight for weight, is lower in calories than sweetcorn kernels and maintains its crunchy texture in this recipe.

BAKED PEAR
with almond crumble

Preparation time: 10 minutes
Cooking time: 20 minutes
Serves 4

75 g (3 oz) wholemeal flour
60 g (2½ oz) ground almonds
75 g (3 oz) light brown sugar
60 g (2½ oz) butter
4 pears, unpeeled, quartered, cored and sliced lengthways
juice of 1 lime
2 tablespoons flaked almonds
150 g (5 oz) reduced-fat crème fraîche, to serve (optional)

CARBOHYDRATE 50 g
FAT 29 g
PROTEIN 8 g
ENERGY 483 kcal/2016 kJ

1 Mix the flour, ground almonds and sugar together in a large bowl. Rub in the butter with your fingertips until it resembles fine breadcrumbs.

2 Arrange the pear slices in 4 tall, ovenproof ramekin dishes and drizzle with the lime juice.

3 Cover the pears with the crumble mixture and sprinkle over the flaked almonds.

4 Bake in a preheated oven, 220°C (425°F), Gas Mark 7, for 20 minutes and serve warm, topped with the crème fraîche, if liked.

Nutrition notes
No additional sugar is added to the fruit in this recipe because the crumble topping provides enough sweetness.

Pears are a low-GI fruit. Cooking fruit until soft tends to raise its GI rating, so the pears in this recipe are cooked until only slightly softened. If you prefer them softer, cook them for a little longer.

Using ground almonds in the crumble mixture means that you can reduce the quantity of butter you might traditionally use. In this way you replace some of the saturated fat from butter with healthier mono-unsaturated fats.

CHERRY AND MACADAMIA GRANOLA

Preparation time: 10 minutes

Serves 4

125 g (4 oz) almond biscotti

15 g (½ oz) wheatgerm

30 g (1¼ oz) sunflower seeds

50 g (2 oz) macadamia nuts, chopped

275 g (9 oz) pitted Morello cherries in natural juice, drained

125 g (4 oz) Quark cheese

250 g (8 oz) fat-free fromage frais

15 g (½ oz) plain dark chocolate (70% cocoa solids), roughly grated

CARBOHYDRATE 44 g

FAT 18 g

PROTEIN 16 g

ENERGY 394 kcal/1647 kJ

1 Place the almond biscotti in a plastic bag and use a rolling pin to crush them roughly.

2 Add the wheatgerm, sunflower seeds and macadamia nuts to the crushed biscuits and mix.

3 Divide the biscuit mixture evenly among 4 dessert glasses or small serving dishes. Top each biscuit base with the drained cherries.

4 In a bowl, beat together the Quark and fromage frais until well combined. Spoon the mixture over the cherries. Sprinkle over the grated chocolate before serving.

Nutrition note

Fresh cherries have a GI of 22. This, combined with the nuts, seeds, wheatgerm (a great source of vitamin E and folic acid), a fat-free creamy layer and an antioxidant-rich dark chocolate topping, makes a healthy but luscious dessert.

OATMEAL AND RASPBERRIES

Preparation time: 10 minutes

Cooking time: 5 minutes

Serves 4

125 g (4 oz) rough pinhead oatmeal

200 g (7 oz) reduced-fat Greek yogurt

60 g (2½ oz) mascarpone cheese

2 tablespoons whisky

250 g (8 oz) raspberries

CARBOHYDRATE 66 g

FAT 10 g

PROTEIN 8 g

ENERGY 257 kcal/1080 kJ

1 Toast the pinhead oatmeal in a dry nonstick frying pan over a medium-low heat for 4–5 minutes until it is slightly brown. Shake regularly to prevent burning.

2 Mix together the yogurt, mascarpone and whisky.

3 Assemble the dessert in layers in 4 dessert glasses. Start with a base of oatmeal, followed by raspberries and then the whisky-flavoured yogurt. Reserve 4 raspberries and some toasted oatmeal to sprinkle on top as a garnish.

Nutrition notes

Oatmeal has been shown to help regulate blood levels of fats and sugars because it is high in soluble fibre and low in GI.

The raspberries in this dish contribute to one of your 5-a-day fruit portions and provide a good source of vitamin C, an antioxidant vitamin.

BITTER CHOCOLATE ALMOND MOUSSE

Preparation time: 20 minutes, plus chilling

Cooking time: 5 minutes

Serves 6

150 g (5 oz) plain dark chocolate, broken into small pieces

150 g (5 oz) silken tofu, drained

30 g (1¼ oz) ground almonds

1 tablespoon almond liqueur

20 g (¾ oz) icing sugar

whites of 3 large eggs

1 tablespoon toasted flaked almonds, to garnish

CARBOHYDRATE 21 g

FAT 12 g

PROTEIN 6 g

ENERGY 214 kcal/894 kJ

1 Melt the chocolate slowly in a bowl set over a pan of hot (not boiling) water. Do not let the bowl touch the water and do not let steam form because this will affect the smoothness of the chocolate.

2 Put the melted chocolate, tofu, ground almonds, almond liqueur and icing sugar in a blender and mix together.

3 Whisk the egg whites until they hold soft peaks. Add one-third of the chocolate mixture and stir to distribute it evenly.

4 Lightly fold the rest of the chocolate mixture into the whisked egg whites and divide the mixture among 4 dessert or wine glasses. Cover with cling-film and chill for 2–3 hours.

5 Sprinkle over toasted almonds before serving.

Nutrition notes

Tofu is made from soya beans and contains isoflavones, which are associated with the improvement of bone health and the prevention of heart disease. It is also particularly beneficial in reducing the symptoms of hot flushes in menopausal women.

Chocolate with a high cocoa content is rich in flavonoids and antioxidants, which are also good for your heart.

CHINESE SPICED CITRUS SALAD

Preparation time: 15 minutes, plus chilling

Cooking time: 15 minutes

Serves 4

3 oranges, peeled and pith removed, separated into segments

1 ruby grapefruit, peeled and pith removed, separated into segments

1 banana, thinly sliced

150 g (5 oz) reduced-fat crème fraîche, to serve

SYRUP

1 whole clove

¼ teaspoon five spice powder

rind of 1 lime

1 vanilla pod, split lengthways

¼ teaspoon grated fresh root ginger

300 ml (½ pint) water

TO GARNISH

1 tablespoon finely chopped mint

seeds of 1 pomegranate

CARBOHYDRATE 25 g

FAT 6 g

PROTEIN 4 g

ENERGY 163 kcal/688 kJ

1 Prepare the syrup by combining all the ingredients in a nonstick pan. Bring to the boil and simmer gently for 3–5 minutes. Remove from the heat and leave to infuse and cool.

2 Meanwhile, mix the orange and grapefruit segments together in an attractive glass bowl. Add the banana.

3 Pour the cooled syrup through a sieve to remove the solids, then pour it over the fruits.

4 Leave the salad to chill in the refrigerator for 2–3 hours before serving with crème fraîche and garnishing with finely chopped mint and pomegranate seeds.

To remove pomegranate seeds Cut the pomegranate in half, insert a fork into one half and twist. The seeds should fall out like jewels.

Nutrition note

Bursting with the antioxidant vitamin C, this citrus salad could be eaten as a starter, dessert or even a sumptuous snack.

PRUNES IN MUSCAT
served with pistachio oaties

Preparation time: 15 minutes, plus marinating

Cooking time: 12–15 minutes

Serves 6

225 g (7½ oz) ready-to-eat Agen prunes, pitted

6 tablespoons Muscat liqueur

150 g (5 oz) reduced-fat fromage frais, to serve

PISTACHIO OATIES

50 g (2 oz) self-raising wholemeal flour

50 g (2 oz) rolled oats

50 g (2 oz) unsalted pistachio nuts, crushed

25 g (1 oz) soft brown sugar

1 teaspoon ground cinnamon

rind from 1 orange

40 g (1½ oz) butter

CARBOHYDRATE 36 g

FAT 11 g

PROTEIN 7 g

ENERGY 280 kcal/1184 kJ

1 Slit each prune in the centre and arrange them in a shallow dish. Pour over the Muscat and leave to marinate.

2 Meanwhile, make the oaties. Mix together all the ingredients except the butter in a large bowl.

3 Melt the butter and add it to the dry ingredients. Combine these together and roll into 12 small balls. Add a little milk if the mixture is too dry.

4 Put the oaties on a nonstick baking sheet and press down on each one to flatten. Bake in a preheated oven, 200°C (400°F), Gas Mark 6, for 12–15 minutes until golden and then cool on a wire rack.

5 Serve the prunes with their marinade, topped with reduced-fat fromage frais and accompanied by the pistachio oaties.

Nutrition notes

These small, muesli-style biscuits are packed with fibre, which helps to promote healthy digestion.

Prunes are high in iron and have a GI of only 29.

RICOTTA AND CHOCOLATE TRIFLE

Preparation time: 15 minutes, plus chilling

Serves 4

100 g (3½ oz) almond biscotti

75 ml (3 fl oz) orange juice

1 tablespoon brandy (optional)

200 g (7 oz) ricotta cheese

150 g (5 oz) reduced-fat Greek yogurt

3 tablespoons icing sugar

few drops of vanilla extract

25 g (1 oz) dark chocolate, minimum 70% cocoa solids, grated

100 g (3½ oz) blueberries

CARBOHYDRATE 42 g

FAT 11 g

PROTEIN 9 g

ENERGY 297 kcal/1247 kJ

1 Soak the biscotti in the orange juice and brandy, if using.

2 Meanwhile, beat the ricotta together with the Greek yogurt, icing sugar and vanilla extract until smooth and creamy.

3 Spoon the soaked biscotti into the base of 4 glass sundae dishes. Divide half the cheese mixture among the glasses. Top with half the grated chocolate and then the blueberries. Spoon the remaining cheese mixture into the dishes and finish with a semicircle of grated chocolate. Chill for at least 30 minutes before serving.

Nutrition notes

Chocolate does well on the GI front, and it is always best to choose a chocolate with a high percentage of cocoa solids.

Adding reduced-fat Greek yogurt to the ricotta cheese helps to keep down the fat content.

PINEAPPLE CREOLE WEDGES

Preparation time: 10 minutes

Cooking time: 10 minutes

Serves 4

1 small pineapple, about 1.25 kg (2½ lb)

1 tablespoon dark rum

juice of 1 lime

15 g (½ oz) sesame seeds

CARBOHYDRATE 32 g

FAT 3 g

PROTEIN 2 g

ENERGY 159 kcal/679 kJ

1 Cut the pineapple lengthways, first in half and then into quarters, leaving the leaves intact. The wedges should be about 1 cm (½ inch) thick, so it may be necessary to divide them again.

2 Mix together the dark rum and lime juice and sprinkle the mixture over the pineapple slices.

3 Toast the pineapple under a preheated hot grill for 8–10 minutes, turning to ensure even cooking.

4 Serve sprinkled with sesame seeds.

Nutrition note
Sesame seeds are rich in protein, iron and zinc and help to bring down the GI rating of this dessert.

LAYERED STRAWBERRIES
with mint, crème fraîche and pecans

Preparation time: 15 minutes

Cooking time: 1 minute

Serves 4

30 g (1¼ oz) pecan nuts, roughly chopped, reserving 4 halves

250 ml (8 fl oz) reduced-fat crème fraîche

1 tablespoon clear honey

1 kiwifruit, peeled and sliced

175 g (6 oz) strawberries, sliced, reserving 4 unsliced with leaves

2 tablespoons shredded mint, plus 4 small mint sprigs

CARBOHYDRATE 13 g

FAT 15 g

PROTEIN 4 g

ENERGY 196 kcal/813 kJ

1 Dry-roast the chopped pecans for 1 minute in a heavy-based pan and allow to cool.

2 Next, mix the crème fraîche with the honey and kiwifruit.

3 Layer the strawberries, shredded mint, chopped pecans and crème fraîche in 4 dessert glasses. Repeat the layers and decorate the top with the reserved pecan halves, whole strawberries and sprigs of mint. Serve chilled.

Nutrition note
Strawberries contain more vitamin C than any other berry.

BAKED SAFFRON PEACHES
with mango and cream

Preparation time: 15 minutes

Cooking time: 15 minutes

Serves 4

2 large, slightly under-ripe peaches, halved and pitted

15 g (½ oz) pistachios, halved

a few saffron threads

a few drops almond extract

30 g (1¼ oz) crunchy oat cereal

2 tablespoons orange juice

5 cm (2 inch) cinnamon stick, broken into 8 pieces

TO SERVE

75 ml (3 fl oz) single cream

½ slightly under-ripe mango, thinly sliced

1 teaspoon grated dark chocolate (optional)

CARBOHYDRATE 16 g

FAT 6 g

PROTEIN 3 g

ENERGY 130 kcal/547 kJ

1 Scoop some of the peach out of the peach halves and chop this finely. Put the halved peaches, skin side down, in a lightly oiled baking dish.

2 Mix together the chopped peach flesh, pistachios, saffron, almond extract, oat cereal and orange juice. Spoon this mixture carefully into the peach halves.

3 Push the cinnamon stick pieces into the peach halves. Bake the peaches uncovered in a preheated oven, 180°C (350°F), Gas Mark 4, for 15 minutes.

4 Carefully arrange one peach half on each dessert plate and pour some of the cream over one side of the peach. Serve with mango slices and a sprinkling of chocolate (if using).

Nutrition note

Choosing slightly under-ripe fruit helps to keep the GI low. The peaches would normally be baked in the oven for 20–25 minutes, but the softer the cooked fruit, the higher the GI, so this recipe bakes the fruit until they are just cooked.

SIZZLING BANANAS
with orange rind and pistachios

Preparation time: 5 minutes
Cooking time: 5 minutes
Serves 4

30 g (1¼ oz) butter
4 bananas, halved lengthways
rind and juice of 1 large orange
2 tablespoons chopped pistachio nuts
3 tablespoons reduced-fat Greek yogurt, to serve

CARBOHYDRATE 28 g
FAT 11 g
PROTEIN 5 g
ENERGY 230 kcal/960 kJ

1   Melt the butter gently in a large, nonstick frying pan, taking care not to let it brown. Add the bananas, cut side down, and cook for 1–2 minutes, using 2 wooden spoons to turn them over.

2   Add the orange rind and pistachios, increasing the heat a little, so that the bananas brown and crisp on the outside.

3   Just before serving, drizzle in the orange juice and serve, still sizzling, with the yogurt.

Nutrition note
Both the nuts and the orange help to lower the glycaemic value of this dessert.

PLUM AND PEACH BRUSCHETTA

Preparation time: 15 minutes, plus marinating

Cooking time: 25 minutes

Serves 4

4 peaches, skinned, halved and pitted

4 large red plums, halved and pitted

50 ml (2 fl oz) brandy

15 g (½ oz) unsalted butter

4 slices sourdough bread, each about 40 g (1½ oz) and 1.5 cm (¾ inch) thick

TO SERVE

1 vanilla pod, seeds scraped out

150 g (5 oz) reduced-fat crème fraîche

CARBOHYDRATE 39 g

FAT 10 g

PROTEIN 6 g

ENERGY 287 kcal/1208 kJ

1 Put the peach and plum halves in a bowl with the brandy and marinate for 20 minutes.

2 Mix the vanilla seeds into the crème fraîche. Leave to infuse.

3 Butter each slice of bread on one side and lay in a large ovenproof dish. On each piece of bread press 2 halves of peach, cut side down. Add plums, cut side up, to the bread and pour on any juices from the bowl.

4 Bake in a preheated oven, 200°C (400°F), Gas Mark 6, for 25 minutes. The bread should be crisp on the edges and the fruit cooked. Serve with the vanilla crème fraîche.

Nutrition note

Fruit is high in the antioxidant vitamins A and C, which are beneficial for heart health and may help to prevent cancer.

HOT BERRIES
with orange cream

Preparation time: 15 minutes

Cooking time: 8 minutes

Serves 4

150 ml (¼ pint) reduced-fat Greek yogurt

125 ml (4 fl oz) single cream

1 egg yolk

1 teaspoon orange-blossom water

1 orange, peeled and pith removed, separated into segments

150 g (5 oz) blueberries

150 g (5 oz) strawberries, cut into bite-sized pieces

CARBOHYDRATE 13 g

FAT 9 g

PROTEIN 5 g

ENERGY 143 kcal/595 kJ

1 Mix together the yogurt, cream, egg yolk and orange blossom water.

2 Mix the orange segments with the blueberries and strawberries.

3 Put a mixture of each fruit in ovenproof serving dishes and spoon the sauce over to cover the fruit.

4 Place under a preheated hot grill for 5–8 minutes until the cream starts to bubble and turn brown.

5 Serve immediately, being sure to warn your guests about the hot dishes.

Nutrition note

Fresh fruit is an excellent source of vitamin C and fibre. Creating a recipe from fruit helps to add interest if you're someone who doesn't like munching through an apple.

INDEX

Author's Acknowledgement

A big thank you goes to my friend and colleague, Elaine Gardner, for her creativity and originality in helping me with these recipes.

To find out more about the author and her work visit her website **www.azminagovindji.com**

Publisher's Acknowledgements

Executive Editor Nicola Hill
Project Editor Leanne Bryan
Executive Art Editor Jo MacGregor
Design Ginny Zeal
Photographer Lis Parsons
Senior Production Controller Manjit Sihra
Picture Researcher Jennifer Veall